Good Green Guide for Small Businesses

How to change the way your business works for the better

Impetus Consulting Ltd

D1037799

A & C Black • London

First published in the United Kingdom in 2008 by

A & C Black Publishers Ltd
36 Soho Square
London
W1D 3QY
www.acblack.com

A CIP record for this book is available from the British Library.

ISBN: 9-780-7136-8932-7

This book is produced using paper that is made from wood grown in managed, sustainable forests. It is natural, renewable and recyclable. The logging and manufacturing processes conform to the environmental regulations of the country of origin.

Design by Fiona Pike, Pike Design, Winchester
Typeset by RefineCatch Ltd, Bungay, Suffolk
Printed and bound in Great Britain by Martins the Printers Ltd, Berwick upon Tweed

Contents

Acknowledgements

Thank you to the team at Impetus who contributed to this book: Dave Barton, Mandi Dyke, Alex Fenech, Flo Greaves, Zoe Holliday, Emma Jones, Rachael Knowland, Kelly Lee, Bindi Patel, Will Rivers, Jacquie Taylor, Keith Von Tersch, Joanne Wade and Louise Wollen.

We would also like to thank the individuals who provided our case studies, Steve Clark at Oaklands Garden Centre, David Wheeler at Manchester Rusk Company and Yasmin and Bruce Halai-Carter at First Impressions Last Longer, for sharing their time and enthusiasm with us.

Finally, our thanks go to Lisa Carden and Camilla Garton at A&C Black, for their advice and support during the drafting of this book.

Introduction

Sustainable development is a topic of increasing interest to us all. Environmentally, it is about making sure that we live our lives in such a way that future generations have at least as good an environment to live in – and preferably a better one – than we have now. The doom and gloom reporting of environmental disasters still happens, but we are increasingly also hearing about how people are acting to improve things. Government is committing the UK to reducing our carbon emissions by at least 60 per cent by the middle of the century; big businesses are very publicly stating their commitments to greening their operations, and communities, lead by places such as Ashton Hayes or the Transition Towns network, are coming together to take action on their emissions.

We all need to be involved in making our lives more sustainable: in our homes, our travel and our work. Some of the changes we may make are quite large, such as sourcing nearly one third of our electricity from renewable resources such as wind and wave power, and these will need government action. But others are small, and much more about what individuals can and should do.

Greening your business is about taking the steps you can to contribute to environmentally sustainable development. The first of these will be small, and a series of these small steps will get you a long way. When you have taken these, there are bigger things that you can do too.

If you're reading this, you must be thinking of greening your business. Perhaps you are already clear that you want to do this and are working out how, or perhaps you suspect that it might be a good idea but haven't really thought about it much as yet. Or perhaps a friend bought you this book and, as yet, you are not at all convinced. Wherever you are starting from, this book can help you develop your business to be more sustainable – to reduce your environmental impact and, in doing so, to respond to the expectations of your customers and your staff.

This book is aimed specifically at small businesses. To get the most from it, you may want to read it from cover to cover, or you may find it more useful to dip in to different sections to find the information and inspiration you need. If you are just starting out on greening your business, you will find ideas for simple, low-cost actions in the early parts of each of the main chapters; if you have already taken the easy steps and are looking for fresh ideas, look at the later sections of each chapter as they are aimed at you.

Throughout each chapter you will be directed to key sources of further information on the main topics within the chapter and to some of the main publicly funded sources of assistance. Each chapter ends with suggestions for a first step to take, and also a checklist of actions that you can use to keep an eye on your progress.

Throughout the book you will find case studies and snippets of information about what other businesses, small and not so small, have done. These will hopefully make our recommendations more tangible and also help to convince you that going green is not only the right thing to do but also something that you *can* do.

Chapter 1 considers why you should green your business. The issues of climate change and resource efficiency are explained, together with the benefits of tackling them: money, your reputation, a motivated workforce and future-proofing your business. It is aimed mainly at those of you who are a little sceptical but if you are already convinced you may nonetheless find it a useful resource when you are trying to enthuse your colleagues.

Chapter 2 explains how you can tackle climate change and resource efficiency by taking control of your use of energy, water and other resources. The chapter offers you simple steps that will cut out a lot of waste in the business, and then moves on to consider more involved engagement with this issue through techniques such as benchmarking, development and implementation of carbon management policies, and including environmental criteria in your purchasing decisions.

Chapter 3 offers you a tool that you can use to reduce your overall environment impact: the environmental check. The chapter first looks at how you can carry out a very simple check to help you focus your initial efforts where they can most easily have a significant impact. It discusses the different types of check you can carry out and considers the areas you might want to include in the check. Later sections of the chapter consider how you can in time build on this initial, simple check to work towards an accredited environmental audit should you wish to.

You cannot green your business on your own (unless of course you work alone). Chapter 4 is about how to make sure that your colleagues are working with you in your efforts. It offers practical suggestions of how to engage people, tap into their ideas, and keep them enthusiastic throughout the process of greening your business.

Chapter 5 looks at how you can promote your newly green credentials, to existing and potential customers, to current and future staff and to investors. The chapter covers the types of message you can use, ways to communicate them and ways to tailor them to particular audiences within and across these main groups.

Whatever we do now to tackle carbon dioxide emissions, there will be changes in the climate that result from emissions that have already happened. Chapter 6 offers you advice on how you can make sure your business is ready to deal with a changed climate and resilient to any increased risks that this will bring. It also highlights where there may be new business opportunities for you.

Moving to new premises or refurbishing your existing site offers an opportunity to significantly improve the sustainability of your operations. Chapter 7 looks in detail at the technologies you can invest in to reduce the energy and water demands from your buildings, and also the approach to take should you be in the fortunate position of specifying a new building.

The subject-focused chapters are complemented by three case studies. These tell the story of why and how three small businesses – Oakland Nursery and Garden Centre, Manchester Rusk Co. and First Impressions Last Longer – greened their activities.

We hope that you will find inspiration and useful information in this book, and that you will use it to help you develop your sustainable business of the future.

Chapter 1

Why go green?

Are you already convinced that greening your business is a good idea? Do you know what the main benefits will be – for the planet and for you? If the answer to both these questions is 'yes', feel free to skip this chapter. Otherwise, read on to find out why reducing your carbon emissions and the other resources you use will help to make your business more sustainable . . .

WHAT ARE CARBON EMISSIONS AND WHY ARE THEY A PROBLEM?

We're all aware that climate change is a big problem and that we need to do something about it. If we continue with business-as-usual, the climate in the UK will alter in a number of ways; some of which may be welcomed but many will not.

Temperature and rainfall changes will vary across the country but, by 2050, average summer temperatures could be at least two degrees higher across most of the UK and three degrees higher in the South East. It's likely that the number of extremely warm days – that's above 27 degrees in the South East – will increase by 10 to 20 per cent. Winters might become 10 to 20 per cent wetter (although with much less snow), with heavier downpours more common. In the summer, on the other hand, it could get 20 to 40 per cent drier across the country, with an increased risk of droughts and restrictions on water use, especially in the South East.

Agriculture, forestry, fisheries and wildlife would all be affected by these changes. While vineyards in North East Scotland might be able to produce decent white wine, the country's seed potato industry could be ruined as milder winters allow virus-carrying aphids to survive. As soils dry out and summer rainfall decreases, more irrigation systems will be needed to support crop production. Christmas trees might suffer from storm damage and pest attacks. Cod could migrate from UK waters and be replaced by Mediterranean species such as tuna. New residents might include scorpions and poisonous spiders, and infestations of fleas, wasps, mice and rats that thrive in milder winters could increase.

Tourism could experience both benefits and setbacks from the changes. Rising sea levels and more storm surges would increase coastal erosion and cause problems for seaside resorts. Less snow could spell the end for the Scottish ski industry, and areas of moorland might regularly be closed to the public as the risk of wildfires increased. On the other hand, warmer weather would attract more tourists to northern destinations.

Damage to buildings and infrastructure could prove costly and disruptive. Buildings in low-lying areas prone to flooding might become very expensive or, indeed, impossible to insure and those on clay soils could be increasingly prone to subsidence as the soils dry out and shrink. Transport networks would be more vulnerable to both flooding and heatwaves, causing rails to buckle and road surfaces to melt.

Life in big cities would become increasingly difficult. Summer heatwaves and their attendant smogs make people ill. If they increased in frequency, the demand for air conditioning – and the costs that go with this – would increase massively. Public transport, especially the London Underground, and buildings could become unbearably hot in summer, resulting in a loss of productivity for businesses.

But what does all this have to do with you controlling your carbon dioxide emissions?

In short, carbon dioxide emissions are the main cause of man-made climate change, and most emissions come from energy use in industrialised countries. Each time you fire up the boiler or flick the switch to power up your lights, your PC or your process machinery, you are using oil, gas or electricity (which is generated from a number of fuels including coal, oil and gas). Burning fossil fuels (coal, oil and gas), whether in your boilers or in power stations, results in emissions of carbon dioxide. So, the more energy you use, the more carbon dioxide you are responsible for (unless your energy comes from zero-carbon sources, but we'll come to that later). But why should you be worried about this?

Carbon dioxide and other greenhouse gases help to trap some of the sun's energy in the earth's atmosphere and ensure that the planet stays at a temperature that is comfortable for us (without them the earth would be a frozen wasteland). But we are now emitting these gases at a rate that means the amount in the atmosphere is increasing. It's rather like being wrapped in a blanket and we are increasing the thickness of that blanket. As more of the heat is trapped by the gases, the amount of energy in the earth's climate system increases and this leads to climate change: the average temperature at the earth's surface increases and there are also more extreme weather events like storms, fuelled by this increased energy in the system. To avoid dangerous climate change, global emissions of carbon dioxide and other greenhouse gases need to be reduced by somewhere between 50 and 80 per cent. Those of us living and working in industrialised countries will have to take a bigger share of these reductions if we are to improve global equity at the same time.

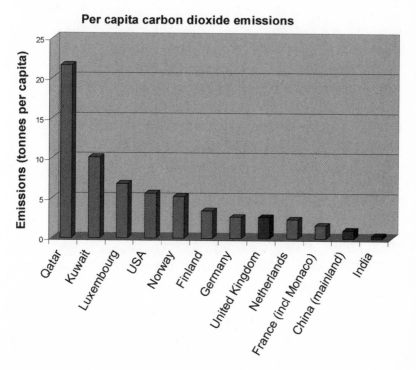

Per capita carbon dioxide emissions

Based on research by the Carbon Dioxide Information Analysis Center.

People often talk about the need to ensure that the world's growing economies, such as China and India, play their part. And, indeed, this will be necessary, but we have to remember the very different point from which they are starting. At the moment, in the UK we are on average each responsible for 2.67 tonnes of carbon dioxide emissions each year, while in China, many people still use very little energy and the average emissions per person stand at just over one tonne per year. In India they are even lower, at about a third of a tonne per year. The chart below makes this difference strikingly clear.

Per capita carbon dioxide emissions

Based on research by the Carbon Dioxide Information Analysis Center.

What about other greenhouse gases?

Carbon dioxide is not the only greenhouse gas, but it is the main contributor to man-made climate change and that is why we focus on it here.

However, some of the actions you take to 'green your business' will help by reducing emissions of other greenhouse gases. In particular, avoiding sending biodegradable waste to landfill will help to reduce emissions of methane.

The remaining greenhouse gases include water vapour, nitrous oxide, ozone, and a range of CFCs (chlorofluorocarbons), HFCs (hydrofluorocarbons) and halons (gases commonly used in fire extinguishers). Unless your business is refrigeration (where CFCs and HFCs have been used), fire suppression (using halons) or farming (where nitrous oxide emissions could be an issue) you won't be responsible for emitting these greenhouse gases so you don't need to worry about them.

WHAT IS RESOURCE EFFICIENCY AND WHY SHOULD YOU BE CONCERNED?

Everything that you do at work involves resources of some sort. When you grab a piece of paper and scribble down a note, the paper and pen are resources, as is the time that it takes you to write the note. Resource efficiency is about how to use and manage the resources you have available to get the most you can out of them.

Sometimes resource efficiency is called waste minimisation. But it's not just about what you put into your rubbish bin, although this is often a good place to start; it's about finding the waste throughout your business and doing more with less.

Essentially, it means using resources such as water, energy and even your workforce more efficiently and making sure you aren't wasting them. The resources you use to produce your final product can include:

- raw materials
- staff time (labour)
- utilities (energy, water)
- consumables (office supplies)
- machinery

It's inevitable that your company will have wastage in all of these areas, so what is the problem with a bit of waste?

Climate change is still our major concern. Everything we produce leads to more climate change gases being emitted into the atmosphere. Think about the simplest thing, say a pen. It is often made from plastic, which is manufactured from oil. To make a pen, first energy is used and, therefore, carbon and other climate change gases are emitted – in drilling for oil, refining it, making the refined fraction into plastic, and forming the plastic into a pen. Add to this the emissions from the transport needed to ship the raw materials, intermediate and final products from well to refinery to factory to supplier and finally to you.

In addition, biodegradable products, such as the food we leave at the back of the refrigerator at work, usually end up in landfill and give off methane. The methane emissions from biodegradable waste in landfill account for three per cent of all UK greenhouse gas emissions.

Our next major concern is what happens to all the material resources that we throw away – the raw materials, consumables and machinery. These will probably end up in landfill. The government reported in 2007 that, in England, 13 per cent of our waste comes from industry and 11 per cent from the commercial sector. It's even worse in demolition and construction businesses, which account for 32 per cent of our waste. And, of course, there are some materials we should never put in landfill (like batteries, which contain acid).

Water is also an issue to contend with, although this varies in different parts of the country. However, living on a small island with a large population, our neighbour's problems are our problems. Water stress in one area will affect the areas around it. In areas in the UK with dense populations, we are already encountering hosepipe bans. London has less water than Istanbul, and the whole of the South East of England has less water per person than Sudan and Syria. The UK has suffered the lowest rainfall, groundwater and reservoir levels for decades and water has become scarce in parts of Scotland, Wales and Northern Ireland as well as in England.

SO, WHY MANAGE YOUR RESOURCES AND YOUR CARBON EMISSIONS?

Climate change is a huge problem and can sometimes seem too big for individuals to deal with. But we are all responsible: in the UK, businesses cause around 40 per cent of total national carbon dioxide emissions; in comparison, households are responsible for about 27 per cent. If each of us takes action to reduce emissions, many of the worst impacts can be avoided. There are also some very direct business reasons for taking action.

Money

The most obvious benefit to you is the money that you are likely to save. Excess carbon emissions often result from wasteful use of energy and as the cost of fuel and power rises the financial benefits of avoiding this waste will increase.

> The Carbon Trust estimates that a typical small business wastes about 20 per cent of its energy. So, if you are typical, you could save around one in every five pounds you spend on energy by taking simple steps to reduce waste. How much would your turnover have to increase to have the same impact on your bottom line?

Savings can also be made on your waste disposal and water bills.

> The Waste & Resources Action Programme (WRAP), which helps businesses to reduce waste and recycle more, has found that companies can typically save up to one per cent of turnover through minimising waste, while manufacturing companies can save up to £1,000 per employee.

Recycling also tends to be cheaper than, or similarly priced to, waste disposal. By recycling more, you can renegotiate your waste contract so that you have fewer collections, thereby saving you money. By using a recycling company you can often make savings on services like paper recycling and therefore ensure that the cost of recycling is unlikely to be higher – and very likely lower – than your current waste disposal costs.

Managing your waste can even make you money. Many types of metal can be resold at a profit. Manufacturing companies may find that their waste, such as scrap metal, is valuable.

Water bills are also increasing and the cost of sewerage and trade effluent charges are going up to meet stricter environmental standards.

Businesses can be paying for wasted water in three separate places. The water you boil in your kettle is a small-scale example of this:

- first you have to pay the water company for the water you use to fill the kettle;
- then you pay the electricity company to heat it up;
- finally, you pay your water company for any water you pour down the drain the next time you come to use the kettle.

All businesses can make reductions in the water they use and save money in all of these places. For manufacturing businesses, these costs can be multiplied many times over. You may be paying to treat water and pump it around your site without using it. You'll also have additional staff costs to accomplish tasks that aren't adding anything to your product.

The same is true for waste. Not only can you save on the costs of materials, you can also save on the time taken in managing and disposing of waste. And, of course, any opportunity to cut down on your costs means you'll increase your chances of gaining a competitive advantage over other businesses.

Taxes

If you use more than a 'domestic' amount of energy, you can also reduce your tax bill. All business tariff energy use, unless supplied from low-carbon sources, is subject to the Climate Change Levy. You can reduce the amount of tax you pay by reducing the energy you use and also by switching your electricity supplies to a renewables-based contract, where the electricity is generated from a natural source such as wind power.

Of course, the government wants companies to reduce their waste as well, so we're also beginning to see financial incentives and penalties trickling down. The government has introduced a landfill tax escalator which will see tax increases year on year. This means that, by 2010, the tax on your waste disposal bill will have increased by £24 per tonne. Further information about landfill tax is available from HM Revenue & Customs (www.hmrc.gov.uk).

But the government isn't just penalising businesses for their waste; it is also trying to help them deal with it. In Chapter 2, we'll discuss the tax breaks available for equipment that will make your business more efficient.

Your reputation

The general public is becoming increasingly interested in the environmental sustainability of businesses whose products and services they buy.

> A 2007 survey conducted on behalf of the UK government found that over half agreed strongly or tended to agree with the statement 'I try not to buy products from a company whose ethics I disagree with.'
>
> A recent report from Ipsos Mori highlighted that sustainability issues are rising up consumers' agenda, and people are becoming more demanding of retailers to keep pace with their changing expectations. The report states: 'half of the online public say they have changed the way they shop over the last couple of years to try and take into account social and environmental issues. Only one in five believes that there is no point changing what they buy as it won't really make much difference to the environment.'

If you sell to other businesses or to the public sector, you are likely to be asked to demonstrate your environmental credentials.

Central government has come up with an action plan that aims to develop the UK's public sector into a leader in sustainable procurement by 2009, which means that the environmental credentials of companies should be taken into account when purchasing or contracting goods and services. The implementation of this plan is increasing the attention paid to sustainability in procurement processes and decisions. As a business, you are likely to be asked whether you have an environmental management system in place: we'll cover this topic in detail in Chapter 3; suffice it to say here that, whatever system you use, resource management will be one key component.

Private sector customers are also looking at the environmental impact of their suppliers. For example, Marks and Spencer's Environmental Policy states: 'suppliers will be expected to minimise their consumption of raw materials and other resources such as energy and water by operating efficiently', while the John Lewis Partnership's Responsible Sourcing Principles state that suppliers 'should minimise energy usage'.

Many big businesses are starting to use their carbon management credentials as part of their marketing effort. Think of the Virgin trains advertising at stations: '76% less CO_2 than car or plane travel', or Marks and Spencer's 'Plan A, because there is no Plan B'. There is no reason why small businesses should not do the same.

Waste and packaging are moving up the news agenda. What started as occasional complaints about plastic bags has turned into full-scale campaigns to eliminate them. In some parts of the UK, Marks and Spencer has already begun charging customers for carrier bags, while plastic bags are now taxed in Ireland. While these are both great starts to dealing with this issue, they are only the tip of the iceberg when it comes to waste. Cutting back in your own business means paying more than lip service to the waste problem. And once you start telling your customers what sort of savings and improvements you are making, you'll find that they'll respond positively.

Over a third of the small and medium business enterprises (SMEs) that the Waste & Resources Action Programme (WRAP) works with said that recycling has improved their reputation in the local community.

For many businesses, their only contact with customers is through the products they sell. Any number of press releases on how you've greened your business won't help if you cover your products in unnecessary packaging. And the last thing you want is to end up in the public eye over an environmental hazard. Topics like hazardous waste only ever pop up in the media when a business isn't complying with regulations, so tackling the waste in your organisation can ensure you don't hit the media spotlight for all the wrong reasons.

Transport is another area with the potential to offer news stories – good and bad – about your business. There are options for greening the fuels you use, but beware of overusing transport (buy locally where you can) or using the 'wrong' sort of transport.

Abel & Cole, the organic food delivery company, has this statement in the environmental section of its website: 'We keep pollution down by using green electricity, by experimenting with alternative fuels for our vans and by never air freighting. Ever.'

A motivated workforce

A motivated workforce is a more productive one, and working for an environmentally responsible company is something that helps to motivate many people.

A survey for the Carbon Trust, released in April 2007, found that three quarters of employees considered it important to work for a company that was actively reducing its carbon emissions.

Staff morale may not be the first thing you think of when it comes to recycling, but it can have a great effect.

WRAP has found that almost half of the businesses who took part in its SME recycling trial identified employee morale as the best reason to undertake a recycling scheme. And over eight out of ten of the businesses found that staff didn't need any encouragement when it came to recycling.

It just goes to show that people are prepared to do their bit for the environment while they are at work, but all too often they don't have the opportunity.

FUTURE-PROOFING

At the time of writing, the Climate Change Bill is making its way through the UK Parliament. Assuming that this bill becomes law, the UK government will be committing itself to ensuring that the country's carbon emissions are reduced by 60 per cent by the year 2050.

To achieve this, carbon emissions from all sectors will have to be managed and this will mean one or more of the following will have to happen:

■ individuals and organisations take voluntary action to reduce their emissions;
■ the cost of emitting carbon increases;
■ carbon emissions are regulated.

In fact, all of these are already happening to some extent. The government is encouraging us all to take control of our emissions and, through the Carbon Trust and the Energy Saving Trust, offering us help in doing so. Costs of emitting carbon are being increased by the Climate Change Levy. Emissions regulation already exists, directly in capped emissions trading schemes, for example through the EU Emissions Trading Scheme, and indirectly through minimum energy efficiency standards for buildings and equipment.

As time goes by and we require ever greater emissions reductions, gentle encouragement is likely to play less of a part as fiscal measures and regulation take over. Starting to take action now will prepare you for this.

Convinced? Or are you concerned that, while a good idea in principle, managing your resource use might be too much hassle in practice?

Turn to Chapter 2, where we show you how you can achieve the changes you want. As you read each chapter, you will see 'help' sections dotted throughout which point you to websites and organisation that will help you implement the changes we suggest and give you ideas for further changes.

Chapter 2

Taking control of your resource use

In the previous chapter we described some of the reasons why you should take action to green your business. Here, we look at how taking control of your resource use will set you on the path to achieving this. This chapter shows what actions you can take to manage your use of energy, water and transport, to minimise your waste production and deal more effectively with what waste you do produce, as well as ensuring that you consider resource efficiency and environmental impacts when making purchasing decisions.

WHAT YOU CAN DO NOW

Why not dip a toe in the water, and see whether some of the simple measures we describe here can make a difference? Perhaps it will convince you, and your team, that there are things you can do.

You can kick-start the process by going to the Business Link website and taking five minutes to find out how to save money in your business. Go to www.businesslink.gov.uk (click on 'environment & efficiency' and then 'identify where you can save money by going green'). This should enable you to come up with some great tips on how to make savings right away, like printing on both sides of the page, turning off unnecessary equipment and lights, and reusing packaging material that you receive. But to make substantial savings, read on.

Energy

A good place to start in your efforts to green your business – and one that can save you money – is to take control of your energy use. The impact it will have on your carbon emissions will also improve your image with your customers and help you to motivate your staff. Act now and you will access these benefits and also be prepared for the impact of increasing government efforts to reduce carbon emissions from the country as a whole.

The energy hierarchy

When considering your energy use, the energy hierarchy offers a good, simple framework that can guide your thinking. It gives you a four-stage process to ensure that your energy use is as sustainable as possible.

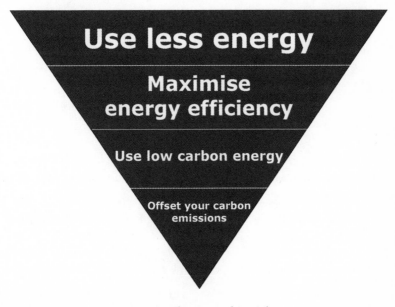

Figure 1: The energy hierarchy

1. Use less energy

The first stage is to ensure that your buildings and processes are designed to use as little energy as possible. It involves things like designing your buildings so that they make best use of natural daylight. We'll look at these options in greater detail in Chapter 7.

2. Maximise energy efficiency

The second stage is about making sure that you are not wasting energy in your existing buildings and processes. We'll show you how to start this process in the section below on 'Finding the waste'.

3. Use low carbon energy

This stage involves seeking to ensure that the energy you do use comes from a low carbon supply option. This could be from renewable energy technologies that you install on-site, renewably-sourced electricity that you purchase from your energy supplier, or the use of efficient supply technologies such as combined heat and power. These options are discussed below and in Chapter 7.

4. Offset your emissions

Once you have done all you can to reduce your demand for energy and to meet the remaining demand from low carbon sources, you are likely to find that your energy use still results in some emissions of carbon dioxide. You may decide to implement the final step of the energy hierarchy and offset these remaining emissions by funding the reduction of emissions elsewhere. We'll discuss carbon offsetting in 'Thinking longer term' (see page 29).

Finding the waste

Start with the simplest of energy audits. Take a walk around your buildings and look at how energy is being used. Are there some obvious culprits that you can deal with right now?

Your own workspace

Do you use a PC? If so, is the screen set to go into 'sleep' mode when you aren't using the machine? (You can find these settings in the control panel under 'display' or, for newer computers and Macs, in the control panel under 'power options' or the 'energy saver' option in system preferences). Do you always switch off the PC before you go home in the evening? Even better, do you switch it off when you go to lunch or to a meeting that will last an hour or more?

> **Leaving a PC monitor on overnight uses the same amount of energy as it takes to laser print 800 pages.**

Do you have a desk lamp? If so, does it have an efficient (fluorescent) bulb? Do you remember to turn it off when you don't need it? Does the position of the desk allow you to make the best use of available natural light? If not, are you able to move it?

The building as a whole

What about lighting? Do you light a whole office when really all you need on is a desk lamp? If you arrive early and put the light on, do you turn it off when the day becomes brighter? And do you make sure the light goes off when you leave your desk? What about the meeting rooms – do you always remember to switch off the lights when you have finished?

Are you comfortable? If you are too hot – do you turn down the heating or open a window and heat the air outside? If you can't control the heating, you need to do something about this by making sure that efficient heating controls are installed and accessible.

> **By reducing the temperature of a heated building by one degree, you can reduce heating bills by eight per cent.**

Do you and others put into practice the same sort of good housekeeping you might use at home: if you use a kettle, do you fill it with only as much water as is needed for the drinks you are making?

These are just a few of the areas where you may find energy waste and, therefore, opportunities to cut down on carbon emissions. You will probably be able to find many more.

Help

- The Carbon Trust (www.carbontrust.co.uk) has free fact sheets to help you assess the energy use in your buildings or in your processes. You can find it by clicking on 'solutions' and 'start saving'.
- Business Link (www.businesslink.gov.uk) has a section on environment and efficiency, which includes lots of information on saving energy.

Getting the team on board

Your staff can help you to manage your company's energy use. You've had a think about your own workspace and have – hopefully – decided to manage your own energy use better, but you also need to get the rest of the team to do the same. You will know best how to motivate your own people, but here are a few suggestions.

Get them involved from the beginning: ask all the team for suggestions on how energy use can be managed more effectively, and listen to what they have to say.

Can you tap into their competitiveness? You could offer prizes for the best suggestions or you could monitor what they actually do and then reward the team that best implements the energy-saving action of the week (for example, awarding points for all the PCs switched off when people leave for the night).

Are you making good energy management as easy as possible for the team? Are all the PCs set with 'sleep' mode activated? Are you happy for people to dress appropriately for the season/weather so that heating and cooling costs are controlled? Chapter 4 looks in more detail at how you can engage your whole team in all aspects of greening your business, including energy management.

Don't forget to measure it

To really take control of your energy use, you have to be able to measure it. Eventually you will want to develop some idea of your 'carbon footprint' (more on this in the box below), but getting started is about gaining some idea about how much energy you use.

Your carbon footprint

This is the total amount of carbon dioxide emissions that you (or your company) are responsible for over the course of a year. It is similar to an ecological footprint, which is discussed in more detail in Chapter 3.

For a business, it will usually include emissions from use of fuels both at the business's premises and in vehicles used by the business.

A more complete footprint will also include emissions from staff travelling to and from work and emissions from public transport when people use this in the course of their work.

Some companies may choose to assess their true impact by including emissions from the manufacture of goods they use during the course of their business and also from the use of any products they sell to customers. This would involve measuring the emissions generated through average use of the product.

Do you know how much energy you use and how this varies throughout the day, the week and the year? You may already have an energy management system that gives you this information – but are you paying attention to what it is telling you?

Half-hourly metering of energy use may be justified if you have complex processes which use lots of energy and that you want to keep a close eye on. Your energy supplier can tell you how much an upgrade to this type of meter will cost and you can find out more about metering in Chapter 7. But measuring your energy use does not have to be that complicated if you don't need it to be. Dig out your fuel bills and have a good look at them. How much is energy use costing you? How much money could you save by cutting out that 20 per cent waste?

Once you have the basic information about your energy use, you can estimate your annual carbon emissions. It's not necessary to gather any information on how much carbon is emitted for every unit of energy you use: there are freely available carbon calculators that will do this for you.

Has your energy use (the units of fuel used, not the cost) increased over time? Does this make sense (for example, because you have expanded) or are there changes that you cannot explain?

Do you need more information than your bills are giving you? Get someone to read the meters once a week for the next few months: this way, you can see the effect of energy management changes you make and report these to the team.

Help
- The Carbon Trust (www.carbontrust.co.uk) offers a free online carbon calculator to help you translate your energy use into carbon emissions. You can use it to get an initial idea of on-site emissions simply by looking at your energy bills over a 12-month period. The calculator will also allow you to measure the footprint of your travel and procurement, but you don't need to do this at this stage, as it requires much more information. Click on 'solutions' and then on 'calculate your carbon footprint'.

Renewable electricity supply: a quick win

A very quick and easy way to reduce your carbon footprint is to switch your electricity supply to a green tariff. This will essentially mean that your electricity is generated from a renewable source such as wind power and will therefore not result in carbon emissions.

At Impetus we rent two offices and in each have switched from the landlord's chosen electricity supplier to one that sources all its supplies from renewable sources. The tariff costs us just a few pounds more per month than the cheapest option available. It's less than what many businesses pay because we compare prices every year and it's helping to reduce carbon emissions.

Help
- If you are supplied via a domestic electricity tariff, you can compare the green tariffs on offer from information provided by the energy consumers' organisation Energywatch (www.energywatch.org.uk). On the website, search for 'going green'. If you use more energy and are supplied via a commercial contract, the situation is more complicated, but you can contact the suppliers with domestic green tariffs (see the Energywatch link above) to see what they are able to offer you. Energywatch is set to merge with other consumer groups in late 2008 to become Consumer Focus.

Increasing the use of renewable energy through green tariffs

Electricity suppliers are legally required to source some of their electricity from renewable sources. So, will your choice of a green tariff lead to an increase in the use of renewables or not? Usually not. If you want to make sure that you support the development of low-carbon electricity supply, as well as manage your own emissions, you'll have to look more closely at what your supplier is offering.

There are several options on offer, all of which can give you some reassurance that you are having a positive impact. Some suppliers may:

- offer to invest a proportion of the money you pay in developing new renewable energy generation;
- use part of the money to fund the installation of small-scale renewable energy equipment in local communities;
- agree that some or all of the energy you buy will not be counted towards meeting legal targets.

Finding the best supplier can be confusing. The UK energy regulator Ofgem is working on a new code that will make it easier but, in the meantime, simply ask your supplier: 'are you using my money to go beyond your legal requirement to supply some electricity from renewables?' and see whether you are convinced by their answer.

Transport

Managing your carbon emissions is not limited to the energy you use in your buildings and processes; it also covers the transport you use. Are your deliveries planned to maximise use of the space in your vehicles (and therefore minimise the fuel that your fleet uses)? If you are planning to visit customers, do you combine several trips in one day (this will save you time as well as reducing the energy you use and the emissions you produce)? Do you set an example to your team and use public transport (or even a bicycle) wherever possible?

Sit down with the person who schedules your deliveries, or the team who are out on the road meeting customers. See if they can come up with ways to minimise fuel use by smarter scheduling.

Delivery scheduling: asking customers to help you be green

The food delivery company Ocado (www.ocado.com) employs a number of methods to maximise the efficiency, and hence minimise the environmental impact, of its deliveries. When a customer looks to book a delivery slot, the times when a van is already delivering in their neighbourhood are highlighted in green and the customer is invited to choose one of these times if they can, to contribute to environmental sustainability. When the customer has finished their order, they are invited to tick a box if they are quite confident that they will not be changing the order. If the box is ticked, the company can assign a more accurate amount of space in the van to that particular order, rather than having to reserve spare space in case the order is updated.

You can also quite easily put together a briefing session to remind your drivers that the way they drive will affect fuel consumption. Check the driving tips mentioned in the 'Help' section below to put this together.

Have you considered the way your staff get to work each morning? There are government incentives to make it cheaper to buy a bicycle for commuting use; can you support this by installing a shower and a changing facility for people who would like to cycle to work? You can also reduce car use by encouraging staff to car-share.

Help
- For ideas on how to green your work journeys, look at the tips on the Environmental Transport Association's website www.eta.co.uk (click on 'green driving'). These focus on cars, but the same basic messages apply to business vehicles as well.
- For more information on the government scheme to reduce the cost of

bicycles, see www.bikeforall.net (click on 'tax-free bike buying' in the everyday cycling section).
- Your staff can find other opportunities for car-sharing through www.carbudi.com and for companies in and around London, www.londonliftshare.com.

Water

Chapter 1 introduced some of the problems of our limited water supply. As a precious resource, we need to conserve it and save the energy needed to move it around. But water also has a financial impact because we have to pay for its use.

The first room to investigate is the toilet. According to the Construction Industry Council, simple water-saving devices can reduce the amount of water flushed away by 30 to 60 per cent, so make sure you install water-saving devices on your taps and in your toilets.

It is necessary to learn about your water consumption just as you did with your energy use. Meter readings will help you to identify trends and, depending on your water use, you should read your meter daily, weekly or monthly. Also, check your meter occasionally after everyone leaves and the following day before everyone arrives. If there is a big difference in the readings, you probably have a leak or a urinal that runs overnight. Leaks can spring up from problems with washers, valves and pipework, so check these regularly.

Case study

Burts Potato Chips decided to move to a larger processing facility and took the opportunity, among other things, to audit its water consumption. Based on this audit, Burts will be installing a number of water-saving devices on the chutes of its equipment. All of these measures combined should result in a 25 per cent savings on Burts' current water usage.

Help

- The Water Technology list will point you to the best products for reducing your water use (see www.eca-water.gov.uk).

Waste minimisation and management

The trick to making your company resource-efficient is to work your way through the waste hierarchy (see Figure 1). These five simple steps can apply to any resource, whether it be aluminium, energy, or paper. Paper is a prime example of a wasted resource in most offices and it provides excellent opportunities for savings at all steps of the waste hierarchy.

Figure 1: The waste hierarchy

1. Eliminate – avoid producing waste

Sometimes you may not actually produce the waste yourself but you should still take responsibility for it. For instance, when an employee leaves your company you'll still receive junk mail in his or her name. By appointing someone in the office, such as the person who opens the post, to update the businesses concerned, you can eliminate a lot of unwanted waste.

2. Reduce – minimise waste produced

There are many opportunities to reduce paper waste in an office. Think about your paper filing. Could it be eliminated or kept electronically?

This is particularly common with e-mail correspondence. Most e-mails do not need to be printed out and many businesses already remind their partners to avoid this in their signature lines. What about changing the margins and font size on internal documents to utilise as much space as possible? Also, consider reducing the weight of the paper you use. Photocopier and printing paper is usually 80 grams per square metre (gsm), but this could easily be reduced to 70 gsm. Likewise, look at reducing the weight of your higher-quality paper.

3. Reuse – use items repeatedly

Have you set your printer so that it uses the double-sided printing default? This is a great way to cut down on paper. There is still bound to be some printing that you don't want to double-side, but don't let this stop you from reusing it. A central spot for scrap paper will encourage staff to use this instead of new sheets. You can bring the amount of blank paper going into the bin down to zero.

4. Recycle – recycle items after reuse

Paper is probably the easiest material for offices to recycle but many still struggle. The biggest challenge is changing the rubbish bin culture. A green office will shrink its rubbish bins and enlarge its recycling ones. Tell staff that their personal bins only take recycling and put a central rubbish bin for non-recyclable waste between every five people. Make this change clear to staff and let the cleaners know so that they empty the bins into the right place.

5. Dispose – dispose of items responsibly. Avoid landfill

This is the easiest step in the hierarchy when it comes to paper. You really shouldn't have to send any paper to landfill, but if you do, it's just a matter of putting it in the rubbish bin. However, it's essential that hazardous chemicals are not sent to landfill, and we'll discuss ways of disposing of these later. Remember that every business, even offices, will have some items that require responsible disposal, including cleaning products, computer equipment and batteries. Check the labels to find out how you should dispose of them and contact the manufacturer if it's unclear.

Case study

Kingsmead Carpets in Ayrshire has joined up with its local waste minimisation club to cut out cardboard and plastic waste. As a result of reduced landfill charges and earning money from the products recycled, Kingsmead has reduced its waste disposal costs by 53 per cent.

Help

■ The Envirowise website (www.envirowise.gov.uk) is full of tailored information for many business sectors. Its publication 'Waste minimisation for managers' includes lots of useful tips as well as a waste opportunity checklist. You can find this through the search tool.

Dealing with waste

We have outlined the five steps you can take to deal with your waste effectively, but there are several points to keep in mind when actually disposing of waste. You will need an effective way of separating the different types of waste that your business produces. Ideally, you would have separate areas or receptacles for recycling, landfill waste and food waste. Within your recycling area, you might have separate containers for paper/cardboard, plastic, glass, wood, textiles, etc. In reality, you may not have space for so many different types of material. As long as you can separate your recyclable material from landfill waste, you will be making a strong start.

Once you have identified the different receptacles you will be using, make sure you label them clearly. Explain the labels to everyone who works there to ensure that everyone understands what sort of waste is allowed in each bin. In particular, there are many different types of plastic containers, so find out which ones your recycling company will accept and communicate this to your staff via the label. Illustrations can help people to quickly identify the correct bin.

If space is at a premium, there are ways to limit how much your waste takes up. Flattening cardboard or breaking down off-cuts of plywood makes it much easier to store waste until it can be picked up by the recycling company.

Help

- You can use this website set up by WRAP (Waste & Resources Action Programme) to find a recycling company near you: www.recycleatwork.org.uk.

- WRAP can also help if you are looking to sell scrap metal or buy recycled products for manufacturing processes. Visit its main website (www.wrap.org.uk) and click on the tab along the top for 'businesses', then down the left-hand sidebar, click on 'buying and selling recycled materials'.

- If you're looking to recycle printer cartridges and mobile phones, try Recycling Appeal (www.recyclingappeal.com). Not only will they help you dispose of some of your trickier waste, but it also gives money back to charities.

Purchasing

Following the waste hierarchy should result in less purchasing overall in your business, but it won't eliminate everything, so it's important to consider ways to reduce the environmental impact of all business purchasing. We'll be discussing this in more detail in 'Thinking longer term' (see page 29), but you can immediately start reducing the energy and waste associated with new purchases.

Energy

One of the simplest ways of reducing your carbon emissions is to buy energy-efficient equipment.

Once you reach this stage in your carbon emissions reduction journey, you will have a pretty good idea about where your energy usage comes from, and you may want to concentrate first on replacing the equipment that uses the most energy: your process machinery or your IT equipment, for example. It is usually quite straightforward to find out how much energy is used by the different alternatives within each equipment type as this information should be included on the specification. You might simply decide to buy the one that uses the least energy, regardless of other factors.

However, it is unlikely that your decision will be as simple as this, as energy use will be one of many factors influencing your decision. Nonetheless, including it in your criteria will usually mean that you choose a product which uses less energy, leading to lower carbon emissions (and of course, lower energy bills).

Cost is likely to be high on your criteria, so you may be concerned about the higher prices of more efficient equipment. Well, 'more efficient' does not always mean 'more expensive'. But if a more efficient product is more expensive, weigh up whether the likely savings on your fuel bills will be worth more to you than the extra money that you will have to pay out up-front.

Waste

Money will not be your only consideration when you try to purchase sustainably. Think about what you will do with your purchases when they have no further use to you. How easy will they be to recycle? Will the manufacturer provide this facility? Toner cartridges are good examples of products which now have a reuse market that barely existed ten years ago. With the introduction of the Waste Electrical and Electronic Equipment (WEEE) Regulations, producers of electrical and electronic equipment will be responsible for disposal costs at the end of the equipment's life. For products where you still have to take responsibility for disposal, you'll also want to know how easily they can be disassembled. This will make it easier to separate out those parts that can be reused or recycled.

When it comes to recycling, you'll want to make sure you're creating a demand for recycled products as well as supply. This can be trickier than you think as there are two different types of 'recycled material':

■ pre-consumer or post-industrial waste
■ post-consumer waste

Pre-consumer waste refers to material that has been wasted during the manufacturing process, like off-cuts of wood or sawdust which are often used in paper production. Post-consumer waste refers to materials that are recycled after someone has bought the product, like the paper you send for recycling. Obviously, businesses should be trying to avoid as much pre-consumer waste as possible, but inevitably some will be produced. So there needs to be a market for both types of recycled material, but you should give preference to products high in post-consumer waste.

Sometimes this information may not be obvious, so check with your supplier. For instance, recycled materials have been part of the process for making brown envelopes for such a long time that many manufacturers don't bother to advertise it. That is changing as environmental concerns move up the agenda, but check if you are unsure.

Help

- The Recycled Products Guide can help you find recycled products: www.recycledproducts.org.uk.
- You might also try your local Freecycle (www.freecycle.org) group which uses an email list to find homes for unwanted items and keeps them out of the landfill.

THINKING LONGER TERM

Hopefully, these initial steps will have demonstrated that there are measures you can take which are not too difficult to implement and that the end result is worth the effort. Assuming this is true, it is time to think about more comprehensive and longer-term plans.

So far we've identified some of the quick wins that you can make on energy, transport, water, waste and purchasing. Now let's look at other ways to identify inefficiency in your business that may take more time to implement or have longer paybacks. To be a truly green business, though, you have to embed the ideas of the waste hierarchy and carbon management into everyday practice. This requires a strategic approach to resource efficiency. Chapter 3, which explains how to perform an environmental check, will set up a strong base for this type of approach. We'll discuss some of the techniques specific to these areas that will also lead to a well-thought-out approach.

Collecting baseline data and benchmarking

To use resources efficiently, you need to know what resources you are using in the first place. You'll want to gather information on *what* is coming into your business and *how much* of it. Talk to the person who looks after the money and look at bills and invoices. (If you've already looked at your energy bills, then you've made a start on this.) An Excel spreadsheet is often the best way to view and analyse the data that you come up with. You can then compare this data with what is leaving the business, in terms of products and waste, to determine how much of each resource you are wasting.

Help

■ Envirowise provides a basic spreadsheet for offices through its Green Officiency Challenge toolkit. You can order one of these through its website: www.envirowise.gov.uk.

Developing a carbon management policy and action plan

Preparing a statement of your carbon management policy will help your staff to understand what you are trying to achieve (and perhaps why) and is also a good way to show others that you are one of the 'good guys'.

What should your statement include? It's quite simple: just a clear description of what you want to achieve. If you think it would help, you can also state why you want to do this.

The PR value of a carbon management policy and action plan can be seen by looking at what some of the UK's household names are doing. For example, Marks & Spencer has a whole website dedicated to its 'Plan A' (http://plana. marksandspencer.com/) and on this you can find very clear statements of its policy aims for climate change and other environmental and social issues, including:

'The five pillars represent the five key areas where we believe we can make our business both more sustainable and kinder to the environment. These five areas are: Climate Change, Waste, Sustainable Raw Materials, Health and being a Fair Partner.

Each pillar has its own goal. By 2012 we aim to:

■ *Become carbon neutral*
■ *Send no waste to landfill*
■ *Extend sustainable sourcing*

- *Help improve the lives of people in our supply chain*
- *Help customers and employees live a healthier life-style'*

And you don't have to be a big company to write a statement of your carbon-management aims. Here is our policy aim:

'The aim of this strategy is to enable Impetus Consulting Ltd to become a carbon neutral organisation.'

Your policy can move on from the aims to set a series of objectives. These are ours.

'The objectives of the strategy are to:

- *measure Impetus Consulting Ltd's carbon emissions;*
- *benchmark this result against relevant indicators;*
- *examine the scope for reducing the company's carbon emissions and using offsetting techniques where necessary;*
- *draw up a realistic plan of action to implement recommendations; and*
- *make provision for the ongoing monitoring and review of progress towards meeting action plan targets as well as the strategy's overall aim.'*

The next step is to turn these objectives into a set of actions that you can implement. Developing this action plan might seem rather daunting, but don't forget that you can simply build on the start you have already made (remember 'What you can do now?' a few pages ago). There are also tools that will help you.

The action plan can also be used to define some more positive messages about your company. Virgin trains is happy to publicise the actions it is taking – and planning to take – under its green policy on the company website (www.virgintrains.co.uk; see the 'about us' tab). These include the following, aimed at managing the company's carbon emissions.

- *'We currently purchase 20% of our electricity at our stations from renewable energy sources.*

■ *We have installed multi-functional devices (for faxing, printing and photocopying) in our offices that will reduce energy and paper usage.*

■ *We have trained our drivers in economic and energy saving driving techniques on both our train fleets.*

■ *As part of our promise to take climate change seriously and reduce our impact on the environment, we are aiming to produce a plan for carbon reduction across the company.*

■ *We are also considering investigating the carbon emissions in our supply chain.'*

Writing down a list of actions you want to take is a good first step, but of course gets you nowhere if these are not implemented. At this stage it's just a list of things that you think will work and will make a difference. Ultimately, you need to make sure that they happen and have the effect that you were hoping for.

Some questions to ask yourself at this point:

■ are you the best person to take forward the implementation – do you have the time?

■ who else might be enthusiastic enough to see this through – do they have the charisma/respect/authority to make it work?

■ how are you going to implement the actions: which come first; where will any money needed come from; who else needs to be signed up to the plan's aims before action will be taken?

■ how often will you review the action plan; what information will you need to collect so that you know whether the plan is working as you intended, and what will you do if it is not?

Developing action plans is considered further in Chapter 3.

Help

■ The Carbon Trust's online Action Plan tool (www.carbontrust.co.uk) puts together a list of actions that could be included within your carbon management action plan, tailored to the size and nature of your business. On the main page, in the 'business support' box, click on 'Action Plan Tool'.

■ The Business Link website (www.businesslink.gov.uk) has a section on environment and efficiency, which includes lots of information on saving energy.

Carbon offsetting

The last step in the energy hierarchy is carbon offsetting. When you have reduced your emissions of carbon dioxide as much as you economically can, you may wish to think about making your business zero carbon. To do this, you will have to ensure that every tonne of carbon dioxide emissions you are responsible for is offset by a reduction in emissions elsewhere. You do this by paying into a fund that invests in emissions reduction schemes (these range from tree planting to investment in renewable energy generation and may be in the UK or abroad).

Offsetting options: the pros and cons

Tree planting schemes

Many of the earliest carbon offset schemes centred on planting trees, either in the UK or in developing countries. The idea is that the tree removes carbon dioxide from the atmosphere as it grows and, provided it is not chopped down and burned, locks this carbon away. Such schemes can provide socio-economic benefits for the communities in which the trees are planted. However, it is difficult to guarantee that the trees will not be felled and also to calculate exactly how much carbon each tree will remove from the atmosphere. Furthermore, tree planting schemes, if not well planned, can encourage the large-scale planting of single species of non-native trees which can have negative local environmental impacts. These issues have led to a decrease in the popularity of this option in recent years.

Energy efficiency

Investing in schemes that increase energy efficiency, either at home or in developing countries, is a very cost-effective way to offset emissions. It can also contribute to efforts to tackle the problem of fuel poverty. The only issue with this option is the difficulty in quantifying actual emissions reductions achieved, particularly from schemes in housing. However, there are well-accepted estimates of savings, and so this should not be seen as a serious drawback.

Renewable energy

Investing in renewable energy generation, either for your local community or for developing countries, has the advantage of combining strong community social benefits with high visibility. On the other hand, some smaller-scale schemes are significantly more expensive than forestry or energy-efficiency options, while very large-scale schemes, such as hydro projects involving dams, can have negative local environmental impacts.

Choose a scheme whose activities you like (you may want to support investment in energy generation in developing countries or you may prefer tree planting in your home town), but to ensure that your money is invested wisely, choose a scheme that has its emissions reductions verified in some way. Schemes in developing countries should be certified, but at the moment you will have to rely on your own judgement for local schemes in the UK.

Help

■ More information on carbon offsetting and Certified Emissions Reductions (CERs) is available from the Department for Environment Food and Rural Affairs (www.defra.gov.uk; go to the page on 'climate change and energy', then select 'action in the UK' and, finally, click on 'carbon offsetting').

Greening your transport and travel

You have already considered whether there are simple measures you can take to make your deliveries or trips to see customers more efficient. Other steps you can take that will further reduce the environmental impact of your business transport include:

- purchasing or leasing of cleaner, greener vehicles;
- driver training to ensure that economical driving techniques are understood;
- green travel planning, which can cover just business travel or be extended to cover journeys to and from work.

As with all other purchasing decisions, try to include environmental criteria in your decisions on company vehicles. If you purchase or lease vehicles for business use, choose fuel-efficient models to keep fuel costs down.

Also, consider choosing vehicles that run on alternative fuels such as liquefied petroleum gas (LPG) as these have lower carbon emissions than conventionally fuelled options. If you are interested in learning more about alternative fuels for your vehicles, have a look at the Low Carbon Vehicle Partnership's website: www.lcvp.org.uk.

The current driving licence theory test includes a number of questions about eco-efficient driving techniques, but you are likely to employ some people who learned to drive before this element of the test was introduced. You could consider using the theory manual and practice papers and develop a short session for all your drivers in which you teach them about driving techniques that conserve fuel.

If you operate HGVs, the Freight Best Practice programme has a set of useful tips on efficient driving techniques: www.freightbestpractice. org.uk (click on the 'operational efficiency' section under 'publications').

Once you have dealt with the vehicles that you own or lease, the management of your deliveries and work trips, and the driving behaviour of your team, think about how your staff travel to and from work. Earlier we mentioned encouraging cycle use. You can build on this and develop a travel plan for your company. The Department for Transport has developed an 'Essential Guide to Travel Planning' that will tell you all you need to know about this: www.dft.gov.uk (go to 'sustainable travel' and then 'travel plans').

Help

- The Energy Saving Trust provides a range of information and advice for businesses wishing to green their transport. See www.energysavingtrust.org.uk and click on 'transport'.

Going beyond simple water-saving techniques

Looking at your bills and conducting an environmental check (see Chapter 3) will help you to find where and why water is used excessively. Once you have identified the obvious places where water is being wasted, look at other ways to save water. More information on how you might save water by adjusting the pressure is given in the box below. A commitment or target to reduce water, for example 10 per cent each year, can also help everyone to find new ways to save. Training your staff in water-saving techniques or starting a water-saving campaign can also lead to significant reductions. Chapter 4 has more information on setting targets and training your staff.

Help

■ You can benchmark how much water your company uses and compare it with others through Envirowise's 'water account tool'. On its website (www.envirowise.gov.uk), go to 'information and advice', then click on 'water' and 'water tools to help your business reduce water'. Finally, click on the 'water account tool'.

Water pressure

If your water pressure is too strong, it can make leaks worse, so people waste water every time they turn the tap on. Too strong a pressure can also wear down your pipes. Water mains should operate between 2 and 4 bar (200 and 400 kilopascal [kPa]) to meet minimum pressure requirements.

If you work in a tall building, the water pressure in the lower floors may be too strong because of gravity. If you think this may be a problem, have the pressure tested and, if necessary, install pressure-reducing valves (PRVs).

When installing these, make sure you check that any equipment you use will run at that pressure and that you are meeting the minimum legal pressure requirements, which means they need to comply with Water Supply (Water Fittings) Regulations 1999. You can find out more about this from Envirowise (www.envirowise.gov.uk). Also, these valves may affect mixer taps or the thermostatic controls in shower units.

If your company uses a lot of water, as part of your check you may want to draw up a water balance.

Water balance

Envirowise's 'water balance tool' illustrates the major uses of water within organisations. Businesses who use a large amount of water and have multiple water inputs and outputs will find this useful. The water balance tool is based on a numerical account of how much water enters and leaves the business and shows where it is used.

The amount of detail will depend on your own processes. By thinking about your business site as a series of blocks with water inputs and outputs, you will develop an idea of how you're using it. Drawing this in diagram form will make it easier for you and your staff to see how much water comes from the water supply and from raw materials. It will also show how it leaves, whether as waste, steam, product or some other form.

Reducing packaging waste

Newspapers frequently carry stories about too much packaging on products and how consumers can protest by leaving it at the till. Any business which ships out products knows that the situation is more complicated than that. Packaging material is needed to protect products from damage; otherwise you end up with wasted products. But packaging also sells products and most businesses spend more time on choosing the right colour than they do on which materials to use. The result is usually over-specified packaging which is only ever used once.

Compliance with the Packaging Regulations focuses on the environmental impact of packaging materials. In addition to keeping hazardous substances to a minimum, businesses should aim to reduce the weight and volume of packaging and ensure it can be recovered or reused. Packaging should also have a minimal impact on the environment after disposal. Applying the waste hierarchy will help you to comply with these regulations and find the best packaging system with the least amount of waste. It can significantly reduce the amount of transit packaging that you use. However, as you work through the hierarchy, keep this caveat in mind: make sure you aren't reducing waste at the expense of damaging products.

1. Eliminate

Look at what goes into producing your packaging. Can you reduce the amount of materials or energy needed to produce it?

2. Reduce

How about getting rid of unnecessary layers? You may need to look at how you handle your products to make cuts here.

3. Reuse

Could you reuse your packaging? For example, if your delivery vehicles return to the warehouse empty, could they be returning the outer boxes of your products for reuse? Opportunities for reuse may be in conflict with your attempts to reduce waste. For example, you may have to strengthen your boxes so that you can reuse them, which will require additional materials. So think about what the optimal solution will be. If using your packaging material once is the optimal solution, then use the least amount of packaging required to protect the product.

4. Recycle

What happens to your packaging after its final use? Make sure that as much as possible can be recycled or composted (in the case of biodegradable packaging) and provide clear instructions on how to do this. In some circumstances you may even want to provide your own service to get it to a recycling centre. And of course, don't forget to use as much recycled material as you can in the first place. Not only do you need a supply of recycled material, you also need to create demand for it.

5. Dispose

Some packaging can't be recycled, so make sure this can be disposed of easily. Clear instructions for disposal are important, but think also about the materials you use. Could these be disposed of in an incineration plant instead of going to landfill? An incineration plant which recovers energy will give your packaging waste another purpose even when you and your customers are done with it.

You can find savings by changing the way your packaging material is used. Look at all of the layers of packaging on a product. For example, there will be display packaging directly around the product; then there's the box that all of the products travel in. If you focus solely on the display packaging for your product, you may find you're using more material than is necessary during distribution. So, you could reduce the material in the distribution boxes, as the display packaging provides sufficient protection to the product.

Also, consider the three main stages for any package: packing; handling and distribution; and use and disposal. During the packing phase, are you using space as efficiently as possible or do you add filler to protect the product? When handling and distributing the product, are you using more material than necessary to protect it? Think, too, about how the customer will use and dispose of the packaging. Look for opportunities to make sure it is reused or recycled.

Help
- WRAP (www.wrap.org.uk) offers two tools to help you improve your packaging. The International Packaging Study contains a database of nearly 200 examples of packaging innovations. The Guide to Evolving Packaging Design provides ideas, tips and practical tools to redesign your packaging. You can find both of these by selecting the 'retail' tab.

Case study
B&Q worked with packaging consultants Outpace to develop a new plastic 'Carrierpac' for delivering kitchen worktops, replacing the traditional cardboard. The Carrierpac uses about 45 per cent recycled content and can also be recycled at the end of its life. B&Q wanted to move away from single-use packaging for deliveries and, during phase one of the trial, the same Carrierpac was used 18 times. Also, there was no reported damage to the worktops in transit, which meant a huge saving on a product that

is often rejected due to scratches and dents. If B&Q uses this new packaging for all its kitchen worktops, it could save 1,100 tonnes of waste per year on packaging alone. If all kitchen manufacturers and retailers followed this example, an estimated 5,000 tonnes of packaging waste could be saved each year.

Mapping your waste

Manufacturing businesses may want to draw up a process map to investigate their waste. This is a map which contains all of your inputs and outputs, taking into account things like packaging material (not only for your own products but also for any supplies you use) and effluent. It should include an estimate of how much waste you are producing. Your finance department can help you to estimate how many products are coming in and how much waste is going out, for instance in a skip or as trade effluent.

Once you have the process mapped out, including how much is being used and leaving your site as a product, decide how often you will monitor your waste and who will be responsible for this.

Help

■ Envirowise has more information on mapping your waste: www.envirowise.gov.uk.

Hazardous waste

Hazardous waste, or special waste as it's referred to in Scotland, is any substance that harms health or the environment. If your business produces hazardous waste, you probably already have systems in place to deal with this. These systems are required by the Hazardous Waste Directive, which includes a list of regulated products called the European Waste Catalogue. You can look at a downloadable copy of this on the Environment Agency website (www.environment-agency.gov.uk) by searching for 'European waste catalogue'.

You can also apply the waste hierarchy to hazardous waste but, in this instance, you should spend proportionately more time on stage one (elimination) and stage three (reuse). Improving the design of products will allow you to use fewer chemicals.

The International Union of Pure and Applied Chemistry has specific guidelines on 'green chemistry', which it describes as 'The invention, design, and application of chemical products and processes to reduce or to eliminate the use and generation of hazardous substances.' The Envirowise website (www.envirowise.gov.uk) has a publication called 'Resource efficiency through green chemistry' which will give you more information on the 12 principles of green chemistry.

You may also find that you could be recovering more of your hazardous waste for reuse than you currently do. Look closely at damaged or faulty products that are currently thrown out. Could you recover hazardous materials from them to use in other products?

Help

- Wasteonline provides useful information sheets on waste legislation such as the Hazardous Waste Directive. You can find these by clicking on 'information sheets' on its website (www.wasteonline.org.uk) and selecting 'legislation affecting waste and recycling'.
- Business Link provides a self-assessment tool on complying with environmental regulations on its website: www.businesslink.gov.uk (click on 'environment & efficiency', then 'waste and hazardous substances' and finally 'assess your environmental compliance').

Considering the environment in your purchases

We have looked at resource efficiency within your own company and how you can meet your customers' expectations by greening your operations. But you are a customer, too, and now we turn to the purchasing decisions you make. Your supply chain consists of other businesses, all of which in an ideal world would be concentrating on the same issues that you are. But that day hasn't come yet, so in the meantime green businesses can use their role as consumers to get everyone thinking about these issues.

There are three key areas that businesses will automatically consider when making a purchase:

- is it fit for the purpose?
- is it providing value for money?
- is it safe?

To make your purchases sustainable, there are a number of other considerations, which are an extension of these three areas. We've already touched on the carbon emissions associated with operating products such as IT equipment and products used in manufacturing processes, as well as whether the products can be recycled after use. Other factors in your purchasing decision should be:

- whole life costing
- running costs, durability and upgradeability
- embodied energy
- toxicity

Start by looking at a product's value for money beyond its initial purchase price. This is often called 'whole life costing' or 'life cycle costing' and it's a way of accounting for all the costs associated with a product. The first step is spreading the cost on the price tag across the amount of time you expect to use the product. For example, if the hard drive on that new computer you want to purchase will stop working after a couple years, how cost effective is it? Accountants use the term 'annualised cost' to identify how much a product will cost you for each year that you can use it.

Example

You have two computers: Computer A is priced at £600 and Computer B is priced at £800. You have previously used computers of both makes in the office and Computer A's brand lasted three years while Computer B's brand lasted five years. Looking at the annualised cost:

Computer A = £600 divided by 3 years
Computer B = £800 divided by 5 years

Computer A will cost you £200 per year.
Computer B will cost you £160 per year.

On this simple assessment, Computer B with the higher purchase price has a distinct advantage over Computer A.

To produce a whole life costing on any product requires you to look at several other factors as well:

- how much are the running costs?
- how easily you can get it repaired?
- if it lasts for a long time, will it continue to perform how you need it to?

So the running costs, durability and upgradeability of any product need to be considered. For most small businesses, it's only necessary to make a thorough examination of all of these factors on major purchases. Nevertheless, these principles should be kept in mind for any purchase that you make.

The whole point of these considerations is to reduce the amount of products you need to purchase. As we saw in the waste hierarchy, this will save on energy and raw materials. Another way to measure how much impact a product has on the environment is to consider the embodied energy. Embodied energy relates to how much energy it takes to produce a product; it's another form of whole life costing but it uses energy as the unit of measurement instead of money. The three major questions to consider are how much energy was used to:

- extract the raw materials?
- process and refine the materials into the final product?
- transport it to you?

Finally, though in no way of least importance, are the toxic and polluting elements of your purchases. Companies should be looking for ways to eliminate toxic chemicals from their products. These can affect your staff by releasing volatile chemicals into the air, also known as 'off-gassing', and they can also affect employees of the manufacturing company who are often located in developing countries. So ask your suppliers what they are doing to reduce toxic chemicals in products that you purchase. You can find more information on reducing toxicity throughout your business site in Chapter 7.

Help

■ The Office of Government Commerce has a briefing on life cycle costing (which is what this process of comparing the total costs of
· different options is known as). You can find this on its website: www.ogc.gov.uk (search for 'life cycle costing').
■ Greenpeace offers a 'Guide to Greener Electronics' on its website: www.greenpeace.org/greenerelectronics.

Supply chain

Once you've worked on the environmental impact of your own product choices, you may want to take a step that many large organisations have already implemented and start to think about your suppliers' impact. We've already considered the potential for your customers to demand that you reduce your impact; well, you are a customer too, and you can influence the business practices of your suppliers in the same way that your customers influence you.

For example, you could include in your purchasing policies a requirement that all your suppliers should be actively managing their own carbon emissions: when choosing between different suppliers, ask to see their carbon management policies and use these as part of your decision-making process. Even if, in the end, this aspect is not the one that determines your choice of supplier, simply asking the question and including the issue as one of the things that will help you make up your mind will increase the attention that your suppliers pay to reducing their emissions.

You can widen this to cover further environmental impacts. What about asking for a full environmental policy? We'll be looking at how to write your own environmental policy in the next chapter, so why not ask your suppliers to do the same?

Tax breaks and financial help

As part of its drive to encourage businesses to become more efficient, the government has introduced an Enhanced Capital Allowance scheme. When you buy waste, water and carbon saving equipment, you may be eligible to claim back 100 per cent of your first-year capital allowance on the equipment. The equipment ranges from efficient taps to water-efficient industrial cleaning equipment and can even include low-emission cars. To find out if something is available through the scheme, check out the website: www.eca.gov.uk.

Smarter working practices

Are your premises too big? The more space you have the more energy you will use on heating, lighting and air conditioning and, if you are a manufacturing company, you may be using more water than you need.

Even if all your space is occupied at the moment, you might be able to introduce new ways of working that change this. Are some of your team out of the office for long periods of time? If so, do they need a work area each, or could a group 'hot desk' and save you some space?

Could some of the team work from home part of the time? Be careful, though, not to simply shift carbon emissions from your office to their homes. But there may be times when working from home is a very good idea: what about in the summer when the office is overheating and you have fans running – wouldn't it be more comfortable if some people were working at home and you had fewer hot bodies and fewer hot computers adding to the temperature in the office? You may also find that people are more productive if given this chance: you are likely to get a better day's work out of them if they can remain cooler and more comfortable at home.

Introducing 'hot desking' and working from home may free up enough space to downsize your premises or at least enable you to stay put as your business grows. This should reduce the total amount of resources that you use per person on the site.

Refurbishing your buildings or moving to new premises

Are you considering a major refit of your premises? If so, now is the time to ensure you include as many of the technologies we've mentioned as you can. It's also a chance to look at the layout to ensure you have enough space for your waste and recycling facilities.

If you own the building, think about how the fabric of the building itself could be improved and whether you could install some on-site renewable energy generation equipment. Even if you are renting, this is the best time to upgrade lighting and heating/cooling systems with minimal additional disruption to your work.

Are you considering moving to new premises? If you are looking to rent a new property or buy an existing property, check the building's carbon emissions, just as we've recommended you do with any other purchase. But if you are planning to build a new property, you really are in the driving seat. Your architect should be able to deliver a low-carbon building that makes financial sense for you (and indeed should maintain its value better than less efficient alternatives as awareness of climate change and costs of fuel increase).

Chapter 7 gives more information on how to improve the buildings you occupy and what features to look for when choosing sustainable new premises.

Working with other small businesses

Are you worried that you will not be able to keep up to date with the latest news and ideas about reducing carbon emissions? Do you think that it will be too difficult or time-consuming to find the information you need? If so, it's useful to club together with other small businesses to address this issue.

The benefits of working together with other small businesses who share your interest in tackling climate change include:

- sharing the cost of finding out information;
- swapping ideas;
- possibly forming a buying group to negotiate good bulk deals on energy-efficient goods and services;
- more general networking – there may be a new customer for you within the group.

Perhaps you're already a member of an organisation that supports action on climate change. The Federation of Small Businesses supports the government's aim of tackling climate change: your local group may organise evening seminars on the topic or, if they don't, maybe you could persuade them to.

Do you know what your local authority is up to? All councils are considering what they should be doing to tackle climate change, although some are more active than others. Can you join in with an existing initiative, or persuade them to work with you?

Example: Local authority support

The London Borough of Camden supports a scheme to help any business based in the borough to reduce its environmental impact. The service is free and includes one-to-one business visits, workshops and events. See www.betterclimate.org for more information.

Can't find anything in your area? If you are keen to make a difference, why not set something up? Individuals like you can make a big difference. If you're interested in how this can be done, have a look at what Philippe Castaing and the other 'London Leaders' are doing: www.londonsdc.org.uk (click on the 'London Leaders' tab).

Join the club

Previously we've looked at ways to introduce recycling into your business. We also want to work back through the waste hierarchy to find ways of reusing materials on your business site. Using a combination of government and EU funding, a number of organisations have sprung up throughout the UK to offer free help to people and businesses in putting their waste to good use by linking them with other organisations that need the materials. These are designed to help businesses achieve the aims of this chapter – saving money, energy and waste – and offer assistance through events, workshops and newsletters, along with a free site visit in some cases.

Help

- Envirowise (www.envirowise.gov.uk) helps you to locate local waste-minimisation, waste-exchange and resource efficiency clubs. Contact your regional representative to find out if there is one in your area.
- Call your council to see what help it offers.
- The largest organisation of this type is the National Industrial Symbiosis Programme (www.nisp.org.uk) which helps businesses trade materials, energy and water to improve cross-industry resource efficiency.

Example: Hertfordshire Resource Efficiency Club

Envirowise funds the Hertfordshire Resource Efficiency Club from the Business Resource Efficiency and Waste Fund (BREW) set up by Defra (Department for Environment Food and Rural Affairs). Club membership is free and is open to businesses of all sizes and sectors within Hertfordshire.

They can offer you:

- an introductory site visit to assess preliminary opportunities;
- workshops, regular newsletters and a website and forum;
- signposting to other opportunities, like a new web-based materials exchange scheme;
- help with monitoring and resource efficiency; and
- a contact point to answer specific questions.

Example: Zero Emissions Research & Initiatives

Zero Emissions Research & Initiatives (ZERI) is a global network of people who view waste as a resource and are seeking solutions. Under this initiative, breweries in Namibia, Sweden, Canada and Japan are using the waste protein and fibre from the brewing process as a substitute for flour in bread making, and as an ingredient in the substrate for growing mushrooms. This has reduced waste and generated additional income and jobs. More information about ZERI is available at www.zeri.org.

TAKE THE FIRST STEP

Hopefully, we've convinced you that taking action to improve your resource efficiency is a good thing, and have a few ideas of what to do about it. So now it's time to act. Why don't you put this book aside for the moment and begin to manage your resources, right now?

- Look at your energy bills for the past year. You might be able to cut them by 20 per cent. What could you do with that money?
- Have a look at your diary for the next couple of weeks: find an hour somewhere that you can set aside to walk through your main premises and identify areas of energy waste.
- Take a stroll around your site and note down where you keep most of your waste and what sorts of material are included. Does this give you any ideas on how you could improve it? Are there items in the rubbish bin that could be recycled? If you've got a recycling contract, review it to find out what you can send to them. If you haven't got one, check the Recycle at Work website (www.recycleatwork.org.uk).
- While you're on the Internet, have a look at the Envirowise website (www.envirowise.gov.uk) for more information on saving resources. You could sign up to their eUpdate and get in contact with your Regional Manager to find out what services are available in your area.

That's all it takes to get started . . .

ACTION CHECKLIST

Energy

Things to do now	Done
Manage the energy use in your own workspace	
Walk through the building to spot energy waste	
Think about energy use in the transport you use	
Get the rest of the team on board	
Measure and monitor your energy use	
Switch to a green tariff	

Things to do after this	Done
Write a carbon management policy	
Develop an action plan	
Implement it	
Invest in more efficient equipment, using the Enhanced Capital Allowance	
Consider carbon when you purchase goods and services	
Design smarter working options	
Think about energy when you refurbish	
Think about energy when you move	
Join an existing network of others interested in tackling climate change	
Set something up yourself	

Transport

Things to do now	Done
Reschedule your deliveries to save fuel	
Set up a bicycle purchase scheme and install a shower	
Things to do after this	**Done**
Invest in more efficient equipment, using the Enhanced Capital Allowance	
Give drivers advice on how to save fuel	
Develop a green travel plan for the company	

Waste

Things to do now	Done
Look at your waste and recycling facilities for immediate improvements	
Make sure staff know which bins they can put things in	
Apply the waste hierarchy to your office and processes	
Contact Envirowise for more ideas and assistance	
Things to do after this	**Done**
Join a resource efficiency club	
Apply the waste hierarchy to any packaging you produce	
Apply the waste hierarchy to your hazardous waste	

Collect baseline data on the resources you use	
Map your waste	
Make your purchases more sustainable – start buying recycled products	
Talk to your accountant about whole life costing for purchases	

Water

Things to do now	Done
Look at how water your business uses water – check out the kitchen and toilets first	
Fit water-saving devices where appropriate	
Things to do after this	**Done**
Collect baseline data on the resources you use	
Map the water you use	
Invest in more efficient equipment, using the Enhanced Capital Allowance	

RECOMMENDED LINKS

For more information on carbon management techniques and technologies, check out the Carbon Trust website: www.carbontrust.co.uk (its small and medium-sized business toolkit is a good starting place).

If you are interested in green energy tariffs, the energy consumers group Energywatch has more information: www.energywatch.org.uk (go to the 'help and advice' section and look for 'green tariffs').

Once you start making your business more efficient, you'll find yourself coming back to the Envirowise website more and more: www.envirowise.gov.uk. It offers information on all of the topics included in this chapter and has a freephone helpline.

Business Link offers practical advice on the environment and efficiency: www.businesslink.gov.uk.

WRAP (Waste & Resources Action Programme) offers advice on waste in a number of different sectors, including help with packaging design: www.wrap.org.uk. Businesses in Scotland can also go to Waste Aware Business: www.wasteawarebusiness.org.uk.

The Government's Enhanced Capital Allowance scheme offers tax relief on equipment to make your business more efficient: www.eca.gov.uk.

The Energy Saving Trust provides a range of information and advice to businesses regarding green transport options. See www. energysavingtrust.org.uk and click on 'transport'.

More information on alternative fuels is available from the low carbon vehicle partnership: www.lcvp.org.uk.

Tips on efficient driving for HGVs are available from the freight best practice programme: www.freightbestpractice.org.uk (click on the 'operational efficiency' section under 'publications'). For cars, the Environmental Transport Association can offer lots of advice: www.eta.co.uk (click on 'green driving').

Case study 1

The three green 'Rs' lead to business growth

Oaklands Nursery and Garden Centre in Laceby, near Grimsby, is a family-run business with six employees. It has reduced its heating bill, reused water and recycled household green waste and wood products. These initiatives have meant the business can expand and develop new products.

CARBON MANAGEMENT

Oaklands specialises in growing bedding plants and shrubs. Owing to planning restrictions in the area, plants must be grown under polythene tunnels – a highly inefficient and energy intensive process. It cost the business £5,000 a year to heat these tunnels, so staff began to make savings by sealing joints to conserve heat.

The next stage was to implement a more energy-efficient heating system. A homemade wood-chip boiler provides heat to the greenhouses, using wood product waste and pumping the heat underground. A new fully automatic system will be installed in the near future.

RESOURCE EFFICIENCY

By storing and reusing all the excess water it uses, together with other water-conservation efforts, Oaklands has saved 89,000 gallons of water per year.

In addition to water savings, Oaklands has made savings in waste, too. As a result of all of the savings the centre has made and the knowledge gained over 15 years of business, it now has a separate business: ClarkeSon Recycling. ClarkeSon Recycling manages household green waste and wood-product recycling from local councils and other sources. The company turns it into compost or uses it as fuel in the wood-chip boiler.

This also means that Oaklands buys fewer supplies than before. The company rarely needs brought-in growing medium as it produces its own. The plant waste often comes in pots, so Oaklands purchased a pot-cleaning machine so that the pots could be reused.

INCENTIVISING STAFF

Most of the staff have worked at Oaklands for some time and supported the green working changes from the start. Eliminating chemicals and excess water use, as well as producing their own compost, means the staff have a greater connection to the overall process of growing plants. They have a better understanding of the plants and can take greater care of them, so a more efficient system leads to better-quality plants.

The nursery implemented the major changes during the quieter winter months, making productive use of downtime so that staff could do all the work themselves. This enabled them to thoroughly understand the process. For example, the nursery installed its own recycling water system, which means staff can make repairs themselves.

PROMOTING GREEN CREDENTIALS

Oaklands did not actively promote its green changes to customers, but as the changes were installed, they were visible to anyone who entered the building.

Steve Clarke, who owns the business, is a popular local businessman and community campaigner. Customers have responded very well to the green initiatives. They have noticed the increase in quality and hardiness of the plants. As the business now includes ClarkeSon Recycling, customers can bring in their old plant waste. The pot-cleaning process is linked with a local trust and provides work opportunities for employees with learning difficulties in operating the pot-cleaning machines. These employees also learn how to grow plants. The nursery won the Humber Adlow Reward for this community initiative.

Steve has certainly felt the benefits of these changes, personally as well as professionally. Overexertion on a new site project led to a hospital visit and early diagnosis of lung cancer. Steve believes his new business ventures spurred on by customers and their overwhelming positive support has contributed to his successful recovery.

ADAPTATION

Steve has also thought about the effects that climate change might have on his business. He may begin growing all shrubs and conifers under covers to enable a better watering regime. At the moment, only plants are grown under these conditions. The nursery has already made some adaptations. The site is prone to sudden downpours, so water that runs off the polythene cover is collected, stored, cleaned and pumped around the site. This saves the company water and money.

FUTURE PLANS

ClarkeSon Recycling is currently in the process of becoming BSI PAS 100 certified, which is a recognised standard for compost producers. This will mean it can bag and sell household green waste, cardboard and wood material which is collected from local councils and other sources. Currently, the compost is only used at their nursery. This new venture will produce up to 25,000 tonnes of compost.

Now that the ball is rolling, Steve can't stop developing new ideas. The nursery may also develop a food waste composting site to further improve the nutrients in its compost. It has also started collecting waste cooking oil to convert to biodiesel.

Oaklands Nursery and Garden Centre is a prime example of how green initiatives can lead to monetary savings and business growth in addition to the obvious benefits to the environment.

Chapter 3

Environmental checks

The last chapter looked at specific elements of greening your business, based on managing your use of resources. This chapter shows how you can determine the overall impact that your business has on the environment. It also presents a systematic approach to tackling problems by way of a simple environmental check.

WHY RUN AN ENVIRONMENTAL CHECK ON YOUR BUSINESS?

We've already discussed how reducing the amount of carbon you emit and the resources you waste can save you money, as well as boosting your reputation and staff morale. An environmental check, or audit, is a great way of assessing if you are taking up as many of these opportunities as you can.

It is also an opportunity to check whether you are in compliance with laws and regulations. As this book is geared to helping small businesses find simple solutions, we don't go into too much detail about legal issues here. Nevertheless, increasingly, national and international laws and regulations are being developed to ensure that businesses are not damaging the environment and it is important that your business is working within these boundaries. An environmental check may flag up areas of concern which require a more formal audit.

More seriously, some businesses have to arrange an audit after an environmental accident has occurred. However, an environmental check can be a preventative measure which draws your attention to potential hazards or accidents beforehand.

In addition to ensuring you are complying with current laws and regulations, an environmental audit can be used to highlight forthcoming legislation. This will allow you to put systems in place early. For example, new emissions ceilings on certain pollutants will come into force by 2010 in the EU.

You may also have to demonstrate to your customers or suppliers that you meet a particular standard. More and more organisations, especially in the public sector, require their partners to utilise an accredited Environmental Management System (EMS) such as ISO 14001 or the EU's Eco-Management and Audit Scheme (EMAS). While the environmental check outlined in this chapter doesn't attempt to meet these types of standards, it provides the first step towards a longer-term goal of adopting an EMS. We will look at more detailed audits in 'Thinking longer term' on page 68.

WHAT IS A SIMPLE ENVIRONMENTAL CHECK?

So far we've identified opportunities for reducing carbon emissions and cutting back on waste. We've highlighted the major issues associated with different areas of your business and offered some helpful ideas on how to tackle them. Here, we provide a more structured framework for tackling these and other environmental problems.

You may have already taken on board some aspects of a simple environmental check before you bought this book. Have you stopped printing certain e-mails or thought about how you might reduce what you put in the bin? All the ideas that you attribute to running a sustainable business are part of the check. The only difference is that a check looks at them systematically and ensures that you tackle all the different parts of your business comprehensively. But systematic and comprehensive does not mean lengthy and boring. How much detail you go into depends on the amount of time and money you have available.

What we are talking about is a planned exercise that you can use to make sure you're thinking about all of the environmental issues at once. However, it is not a complete environmental audit, although it can be the first step. It does not include important and lengthier investigations into areas such as hazardous waste and duty of care regulations. Instead, it focuses on minimising the amount of resources that you waste in your business, by identifying areas of concern.

Deciding where to begin can be daunting, but our guide will make it easy for you. Carrying out your check involves five main steps:

1 be clear why you are doing it (define your objective)
2 set the boundaries accordingly (define your scope)
3 collect information
4 assess
5 follow up

1 Defining your objective

Your objective determines the 'why'. Why have you decided to undertake an environmental check? Perhaps you want to find ways to cut down on the waste your organisation produces or reduce the amount of water you use in your manufacturing process. You may wish to focus on a particular area of concern initially (for example, you may be worried about a particular process that uses a lot of energy, or maybe you're concerned about the environmental impact of your delivery fleet) and then run another check on other areas of the business at a later date.

2 Defining your scope

Deciding on your overall objective (the 'why') of the environmental check allows you to focus your scope. The scope explores the 'who', 'what', 'when', 'where' and 'how'.

Who

Decide 'who' will be doing the check. If your business already has an 'environmental champion' (see box), then he or she should be involved.

Environmental champion
An environmental champion is the person whose job it is to make sure that the process of greening your business actually happens.

Who should it be? You want someone with a combination of knowledge, skills and personality who offers:

- commitment to the process
- an understanding of what is to be done
- the ability to persuade others

Ideally, a single individual should perform this role, but he or she may need a small support team with the relevant knowledge and/or the ability to persuade different individuals and teams within your company.

It is important for everyone to know that the environmental champion is fully supported by the senior management team.

A support team should include people who are already enthusiastic about the environment, as this helps to keep momentum. They should also be familiar with the day-to-day processes of the business. Involving more than one person increases the likelihood that your check will cover everything.

What

'What' are you going to include in your simple environmental check? Deciding on the 'what' of the scope will largely depend on your type of business, i.e. whether you are office-based, a shop or a manufacturer. If your business manufactures a product, decide whether you will focus on one aspect of the business or conduct a whole life cycle analysis (LCA) of your product. We provide further information on LCA in 'Thinking longer term' on page 68.

A transport analysis may also be appropriate. This might focus on transport within the business – transport of products, goods, staff and customers for the purpose of the business – or it could be widened to include all staff travel to and from work.

The scope of the check will also depend on whether you own or rent your premises. A lease may restrict what you can do with the space, but there are still many actions you can take. In addition, you can always talk to the landlord about your findings as he or she may be willing to agree to changes.

When

Decide 'when' the check should take place and define a timeline. You should avoid particularly busy times of year or day. In addition, decide how often you want to revisit the check. Businesses often choose to review every year or two. If you discover significant problems in one area, you may want to review your progress in that area more frequently.

Where

The 'where' determines the spatial parameters. If your business has more than one site or office, you might want to try the environmental check on your main site first. Decide whether you want to confine your check to the business site or incorporate surrounding areas. For example, manufacturing businesses may want to check surrounding rivers and streams to determine if the business is having an impact upon them. If this is the case, a more formal audit may be required.

How

Finally, decide 'how' you will assess the business. The section on 'What to look out for' on page 64 outlines the basic areas that your simple environmental check could cover. After determining the rest of the scope, you may decide that you need a more formal environmental audit. We've included information on other types of audits that small businesses can undertake later in this chapter.

3 Collecting information

In order to help make the environmental check go smoothly, it is important to gather as much information beforehand as possible. If you've followed the advice in Chapter 2, you may already have collected some of this data, such as electricity, water and fuel bills. You can use this information to determine the business's yearly consumption data. Also, get hold of the floor plan of your premises and determine the size of floor area used. Using both types of data enables you to set a benchmark for your business, as outlined in Chapter 2, and compare it against similar businesses.

This is also the time to review your company's history of environmental action. Perhaps there is a draft environmental policy that was never implemented or an audit performed in years past. Familiarise yourself with any existing documentation on the company's environmental performance and look for areas flagged for improvement in the past.

At this stage, you may also wish to determine your business's carbon footprint, as discussed in Chapter 2, in order to gain a better picture of how you are faring. This will help you when setting targets for reductions. In addition, you could determine your wider ecological footprint. This requires more time and resources than the simple check, so we've provided more information on this in 'Thinking longer term' on page 68.

4 Assessment

There are two main ways in which to conduct the actual assessment of your business: undertaking a walkabout or collecting feedback. Of course, a combination of the two may also prove beneficial.

Walkabouts are a site survey. They involve walking through the premises and assessing set criteria. This can be done by developing your own checklists and survey forms or by using acquired templates from online guidance and audit software. Examples of templates include the Envirowise 'Green Officiency Challenge toolkit' (go to www.envirowise.gov.uk and search for 'green officiency') for offices and the Carbon Trust's templates for assessing industrial sites and energy use in buildings. To find this, go to www.carbontrust.co.uk and click on the 'publications' tab; then search for 'assessing the energy use at your industrial site'.

If time is of the essence or a walkabout is not practical, you can obtain feedback from staff by conducting interviews or sending out a questionnaire. Again, you can use acquired templates such as the ones mentioned above or produce your own personalised forms.

5 Following up

It is easy to complete the assessment and then forget about it, but of course if you really want to green your business, a follow-up plan is vital.

Determine your goals and decide what you would like to implement now, in the near future and in the longer term. The environmental check should lead to an action plan of realistic changes. Changes that you want to implement right away, such as ensuring that office equipment is turned off when not in use, will probably be quick and cost-free, while longer-term goals, such as reducing the hazardous chemicals in your manufacturing process, are likely to be more expensive and take more planning. It is important to prioritise your actions, as some measures may be urgent, for example fixing leaky taps, while others can wait. Prioritising also ensures that your action plan isn't too overwhelming.

Circulate the findings of the assessment to all employees. At this point you may want to gather feedback before deciding on the timeframe for implementing each step of your action plan. Give a clear indication of when you will revisit the check to remind people that action is expected. If necessary, conduct a follow-up check. These follow-up steps will keep the wheels in motion and help keep staff focused on the problems you have identified.

Other types of audits

Issue and activity audits

An issue audit focuses on a specific environmental issue such as climate change or rainforest deforestation. This type of audit is usually more relevant for larger businesses, although it can be used for smaller companies. For example, you may wish to identify how your business is contributing towards climate change.

An activity audit, on the other hand, looks at one activity in your business, such as transport, your procurement process, waste disposal or packaging. Although a simple environmental check touches on some of the same areas, such as the procurement process, an activity audit provides a more thorough examination. You may decide to undertake an activity audit if you require further information on a specific aspect.

Product audit

While a simple environmental check looks at the business's processes, a product audit focuses on one or more commodities that the business produces. It requires a life cycle analysis (LCA) of the product, taking into account its entire history, from the very beginning to the absolute end, including all the players. For example, a product audit of the stationery from a paper mill would look at:

- where the trees are sourced, how they are extracted and their transport;
- how the wood is processed into paper;
- the transport of paper to the shops who will sell it;
- how the paper is used once purchased (for example, are both sides used?);
- what do your customers do with the paper after they use it – is it thrown out with general waste or recycled? You may need to do some customer research to find these things out.

Legal issues audit

A simple environmental check doesn't go into too much detail about compliance with environmental legislation, but it's important to ensure that you are working within the law, and a legal issues audit may be necessary to substantiate this. You should not attempt to conduct this type of audit on your own as you'll need to consult at least one expert.

A legal issues audit may also be required when buying or selling premises to ensure that there are no major environmental concerns such as land contamination. Some businesses will pre-empt a potential environmental problem by performing an audit before selling a property. Potential buyers will also undertake a thorough assessment to ensure they will not be liable for any current or potential environmental risks. Legal issues audits are known by a variety of names, including compliance audits, liability audits, due diligence audits, acquisition audits and pre-acquisition audits.

Legislation
Environmental legislation and regulations are ever increasing. This box highlights some of the major regulations that apply to businesses.

The EU regulation dealing with the Registration, Evaluation, Authorisation and Restriction of Chemical substances (REACH) came into force in 2007. It aims to protect both human health and the environment, in addition to increasing innovation and competitiveness within the EU chemicals industry. Manufacturers and importers will be responsible for managing the risks associated with chemicals and will be required to provide safety information on the substances. REACH will be phased in gradually over an eleven-year period.

There is also an EU Directive on Integrated Pollution Prevention Control (IPPC). Under this directive, heavily polluting industries need permits and must meet set standards. This won't apply to most small businesses, but as some may fall under these regulations, it is important to be aware that they exist.

In the UK, the Environmental Protection Act (EPA) 1990 gives statutory bodies and local councils the power to issue regulations. Waste and clean air are some of the areas that fall under EPA regulations.

Help

- Envirowise's website (www.envirowise.gov.uk) has a tab for 'environmental legislation'. You can choose the subject of the legislation and find out what your industry needs to do to comply.
- The government website www.netregs.gov.uk is specifically designed to help small and medium-sized businesses tackle environmental issues, including compliance with relevant legislation.

WHAT TO LOOK OUT FOR

Here, we've outlined the basic areas you may wish to cover in your environmental check, such as energy, waste and water conservation and whether you could improve your resource efficiency, for instance by using more environmentally-friendly products. We'll deal with the relevant issues under the following categories:

- building
- equipment and supplies
- processes and behaviour

Building

Structure

Step back and look at the building fabric as a whole. What is the age of the property and what is it made of? Have extensions been added? Is it insulated? Does it have cavity walls? It is helpful to have a floor plan of the building with dimensions, as this will make it easier to calculate energy usage. If you don't have a floor plan, measure the floor area yourself.

Temperature and air quality

Find out about the building's heating, ventilation and air conditioning systems. Things to consider are the age of the systems, and how the building is heated and cooled. Are the radiators appropriately placed, and do the systems have individual controls that respond to temperature (called thermostatic radiator valves or TRVs). Is the heating or air conditioning left on when windows are open? Check if staff know how to use the systems and if there is a procedure to turn them off at the end of the day.

Ask staff members how they feel about the temperature. Do they find the rooms are too hot or too cold? It's important to get feedback from several people, as opinions may vary.

Lighting and windows

Is enough natural light coming into the building? If not, is there anything obvious blocking the windows that could be cleared, such as overgrown vegetation? Are the windows double-glazed, are there any draughts and do any of the windows not close properly?

Make a note of what sort of lighting is used, for example CFLs (compact fluorescent lamps) or tungsten light bulbs. If lights cannot currently be controlled individually, should this be changed? Are any lights on unnecessarily? Does your business have a standard turn-off procedure in place?

Toilets

You might not think of toilets as an area to be considered when greening your business, but savings can be made here too, so they shouldn't be overlooked. Your check should reveal if there are any leaking pipes or taps and if spray taps or other water-efficiency measures have been installed.

Check how much water the cistern uses. If it is wasting water (which it will be if it was installed before 2001, using any where from seven to 12 litres per flush rather than the four to six litres used by more modern toilets), a Hippo bag, which is a plastic bag used to displace water, or an alternative should be installed. A dual flush is another option to conserve water. See Chapter 2 for more information on this issue.

Finally, make a note of the products used, such as soap, toilet paper and cleaning products. Switch to environmentally-friendly options if you're not already using them.

Kitchens

Make the same checks as above for leaks and water-efficient measures. Also, check if you have energy A-rated appliances and whether they are used effectively and efficiently. For example, is the refrigerator being used enough to warrant the size of appliance? If you have a dishwasher, is it filled completely before being turned on?

Finally, have a look through the cupboards. Do you have reusable cutlery and crockery? Look at the products you have and what they're made of. Cleaning products in particular can be full of unnecessary chemicals, so consider buying environmentally-friendly alternatives.

Equipment and supplies

Office equipment

Think about the environmental impact of the equipment you use. For example, in Chapter 2 we looked at computers, but you should also consider other equipment such as printers and photocopiers. Where appropriate, are efficient models used? Is equipment turned off when not in use for long periods of time and is there a standard shut-down procedure?

Stationery and other products

Quite often, businesses don't give any thought to where their supplies come from, but the associated carbon dioxide emissions from transport alone can be staggering. Although it takes a bit of time to research new suppliers, by opting for locally-sourced supplies, you will be reducing your environmental impact. For more information on the impact of your purchases, see Chapter 2.

Waste

What happens to the waste your business produces? Do you have recycling facilities and, if so, are such facilities being used to their full potential? Can any of the waste be reused, for instance packaging or envelopes? Assessing your waste can reveal areas where both financial and resource savings can be made.

Your check should also determine whether or not your stationery and other products are environmentally-friendly, sustainably sourced or made from recycled materials.

Processes and behaviour

Manufacturing process

The simple environmental check should include an overview of any manufacturing process that your business uses. Of course, this will vary for different types of businesses, but fundamentally you should be looking at the overall efficiency of the process. Do you know how efficient your machines are and are they left on unnecessarily? How much waste is there at the end of the day and can this be reduced, reused or recycled? Do you use water in the process and can that water be reduced or reused? Chapter 2 has more information on how you can save water and cut down on waste in your manufacturing process.

Travel

As mentioned in Chapter 2, you may wish to include all business-related travel in your environmental check. Are there more sustainable ways to transport your products? If you have company cars, are they fuel-efficient? If you visit clients, could you take a train instead of driving or plan your journey to include several visits to reduce overall travel? Are there instances where you could avoid travel altogether?

In addition to assessing business-related travel, you could interview staff members. How far do they travel to work and what mode of transport do they use? Are there more sustainable modes of transportation available? Are you located on a bus route? Do you encourage sustainable travel by providing access to bicycle racks and changing and showering facilities? Could car pooling be encouraged?

There are vast opportunities to reduce emissions resulting from your business travel. By looking at the whole picture you should be able to find several areas that can be improved. You may want to formalise the process by developing a green travel plan (see Chapter 2 for more on this).

Staff involvement

Asking staff for their views helps to ensure you're not missing any opportunities for savings or improvements to your environmental record, as well as ensuring you have correct and up to date data to work from. It is also a good way of gaining commitment from staff before you ask them to make changes in the way they work. We'll give more advice on incentivising staff and overcoming barriers to change in Chapter 4.

THINKING LONGER TERM

Developing an environmental policy and action plan

Formalising your goals into an environmental policy will make it easy for others to see what you are trying to do, and is one of the main messages that you can communicate to your staff and your customers.

In Chapter 2 we showed you how to develop a carbon management policy and action plan. The same principles apply here: you simply define your goals in broader environmental management terms, and the overall aim is to manage your environmental impact rather than simply address your contribution to climate change.

When you have completed your initial environmental check and identified areas where improvements can be made, you might decide to implement just a few of the quick and easy changes in the short term.

However, in the longer term it is a good idea to formalise the results into an environmental action plan.

Chapter 4 discusses how to involve the team in identifying and prioritising actions. When prioritising, think about:

■ the extent to which the change will reduce your environmental impact – so that you avoid getting bogged down in little details that won't have a huge impact;
■ the money that you will need to invest and the savings that will be generated – you may need to give greater priority to measures that save you money in order to generate the funds for actions that require investment;
■ the ease with which your team can make the required changes – giving priority to a few easy things that will deliver quick results will help to keep people motivated.

Once you have done this, writing the plan should be straightforward. It is in essence a list of actions, each defined as follows:

■ what needs to be done;
■ why it needs to be done (what target will it contribute to);
■ what the outcome is expected to be;
■ who needs to do it;
■ when it needs to be completed by.

Obviously, to define some of the above, you will need to work with the people who will deliver the changes. For longer-term actions you may want to set a series of milestones along the way, as well as the end deadline, so that you can track progress.

How you will organise the list will depend on the best option for your exact circumstances, but tasks could be grouped:

■ by order of priority;
■ according to whether they are short term or require more time to implement;
■ by the building or process to which they apply;
■ into action areas for different teams within your company.

The action plan should have a section that explains how progress will be monitored and states how often the plan itself will be reviewed and updated.

Example

At Impetus Consulting Ltd, we have chosen to focus on two of the areas on which we can have the biggest impact: energy and water. We have drawn up a simple action plan to reduce energy.

The following hierarchy of solutions is advisable:

- *reduce energy use;*
- *use renewable sources of energy; and*
- *purchase carbon offsets to compensate for the carbon dioxide emitted by Impetus in the course of its business.*

We then give details about how we will implement these actions.

Reducing energy use

Although Impetus' carbon emissions from fuel use do not contribute significantly to its overall total, the company still implements a policy of efficient use of energy. In addition, Impetus has a strategy to procure energy-efficient goods such as light bulbs, office equipment and PCs. When an appliance needs replacing, priority is given to an energy-efficient model even when this option may be more costly than less efficient alternatives.

Your action plan should also show your plans for continuous improvement. Our action plan explains how we will monitor and review our resource use.

Monitoring

Electricity, gas and water meter readings are taken on a monthly basis. The business travel log is also updated each month as a part of the process for submitting expenses.

> ### Review
> *Impetus' carbon emissions will be calculated on a quarterly basis and include a review of staff travel-to-work patterns. The implementation of the carbon management strategy will be subject to a six-monthly review.*

Building on the initial environmental check

For some companies, an environmental check will meet most of their environmental concerns and they can rest easy – as long as they keep monitoring and reviewing the situation. For others, a quick check is just the beginning of the process. Or it may be that you had more ambitious plans for your company right from the start. Whatever your situation, there are a number of ways to extend your check and during the review process it is a good idea to think about what your next steps should be.

Environmental Management System (EMS)

So far in this chapter, we have focused on a simple environmental check that you can carry out yourself. But, depending on your particular needs, you might want to consider a more substantial audit or even an EMS, which would require continuous monitoring and improvement instead of a single check. Your objective (as defined under 'What is a simple environmental check' on page 58) should help you to decide which audit is the best one for you to use.

The UN Department of Economic and Social Affairs stresses that all businesses should make environmental management one of their main priorities, to ensure that sustainable development goals are achieved. An EMS which requires accreditation will help you to monitor your performance and make improvements towards a more sustainable business.

You can follow the audit procedures of either the International Standards Organisation's ISO 14001 or the EU's Eco-Management and Audit Scheme (EMAS), both of which are designed to provide ways for businesses to control and reduce their environmental impact. Every aspect of the business is examined, such as management, policies and systems. The environmental British Standard BS 8555 was designed specifically for small and medium-sized businesses and provides a comprehensive but achievable start to an EMS. The standard is broken down into phases and can be used as a stepping stone to ISO 14001 or EMAS.

As long as you comply with the set procedure, you have the choice of doing the audit yourself or hiring another company to carry out the work. Once the audit is completed, it needs to be verified by an independent accredited environmental verifier (AEV) who will confirm that it meets the set criteria. At this point, your business will receive certification providing recognised proof of your business's green credentials that you can share with your clients and customers. Bear in mind that obtaining accreditation costs money and requires a lot of time and dedication.

Help

■ The Institute of Environmental Management and Assessment provides information on the three Environmental Management Systems that we mention: www.iema.net.

Example: Customers like to see high-quality environmental management

Pepper Communications Ltd won new customers and achieved business growth after achieving the BS 8555 national environmental standard.

Ecological footprinting

An ecological footprint of your organisation calculates the area of land that would be required to support your business. This translates your resource and energy consumption into a measurement of land area, hectares per person. This provides a useful benchmark for comparing your business with others, as well as giving you a better idea of how sustainable your business is.

Help

■ Best Foot Forward provides ecological footprinting services through Footprinter – its ecological and carbon footprinter calculator – or through bespoke services for organisations: www.bestfootforward.com.

Checking up on your suppliers

You might consider broadening your scope to include areas beyond your premises and the land next door. Supplier audits are becoming increasingly frequent as more companies are implementing EMS or EMAS where supplier assessments are required. A life cycle analysis (LCA) also requires you to assess suppliers, but there are other reasons why you may choose to perform an environmental check outside your company. Perhaps you want to know if your current suppliers have green credentials or maybe you are making initial contact with a co-producer and want to use it as part of the selection criteria.

How much detail you go into depends on why you need the information. If you are undertaking a complete LCA you may need to conduct a thorough audit. A simple questionnaire sent to your suppliers may prompt them to undertake an audit themselves in order to respond to the questions. Requesting a company's environmental policy may be sufficient for your needs. So, another benefit of auditing outside your company is that you are encouraging other businesses to assess themselves environmentally.

Help wanted

We've emphasised the need to employ an external company for several of these more detailed options and, although our simple environmental check can be done by you, more complicated audits usually require expert assistance.

During your own check, you might discover a serious issue that needs more investigation. Perhaps chemicals used in your manufacturing are finding their way to the nearby stream. Alternatively, you may have found that your energy use is much higher than the benchmarks, but you can't find the cause. In both instances, an expert opinion is useful not only to confirm and identify potential issues, but also to offer practical solutions. And an external company can provide you with bespoke solutions for your business site and circumstances. If you are looking for something beyond the standard solution or considering newer technology, like renewable energy, you will want to enlist the help of experts.

You might decide to bypass your own check and employ an external company as a first step. In doing so you will gain expertise and save time, but it doesn't get you out of all the responsibility for the audit. A successful audit depends on internal co-ordination to oversee the whole process from start to finish and to spend time explaining thoroughly how the business is run.

TAKE THE FIRST STEP

We have given you the tools to begin your own simple environmental check. You may even recognise your business in some of the examples we provided or perhaps some issues popped into your head while you were reading. Why don't you jot down those thoughts now while they are still fresh in your mind? They are a good place to start.

Next, set some time aside to begin the process of your check. It should take less than an hour. This is when you look at your 'objective', determine why you want to do the check, and what you want to achieve. A chat with other colleagues will help you to define your objective.

This will lead you to the 'scope'. Decide the 'who', 'what', 'when', 'where' and 'how'. Once you've defined the scope, start collecting the background information you need to give you the full history. So, dig out the floor plans and work out how much electricity, gas and water you use per area.

By taking these first steps you will be halfway to completing your simple environmental check and working towards a greener business.

ACTION CHECKLIST

Things to do now	Done
Define your objective – why are you running an environmental check?	
Set the scope of your check – who, what, when, where and how	
Collect background information – e.g. utility bills and the floorplan	
Carry out a walkabout or interview staff (face to face or by questionnaire) on:	
■ building	
■ equipment and supplies	
■ processes and behaviour	
Review your findings and develop a follow-up plan	
Monitor your progress regularly	

Things to do after this	Done
Consider working towards an Environmental Management System	
Perform an audit or check on current and potential suppliers	
Hire an expert consultancy to help you with longer-term plans	

RECOMMENDED LINKS

For more information on environmental legislation, check out the NetRegs site (www.netregs.gov.uk) and Envirowise (www.envirowise.gov.uk).

The Institute for Environmental Management and Assessment offers further information on environmental management processes and systems: www.iema.net

If you are interested in developing an ecological footprint of your business, the tools available from Best Foot Forward (www.bestfootforward.com) could be helpful.

Case study 2

Investing in environmental technologies makes good business sense

Manchester Rusk Co. Ltd manufactures sauces and seasonings, employing 40 staff based in the North West of England. Technology improvements have tripled the company's output and ensured some of its energy comes from renewable resources.

INCREASING EFFICIENCY

Premises

Management staff at Manchester Rusk have always been aware of the benefits of reducing consumption of utilities – electricity, gas and water. Therefore, when the company built a new factory, staff decided to incorporate energy-efficient features into the design, such as insulated ceilings, double glazing and an energy management system to control gas usage.

The company continued to make improvements to its premises, including installing low energy lighting in the production and office areas, and fitting sensors to outside lights so that they only come on when required. This has reduced energy use for lighting by 60 per cent.

Replacing existing computer monitors with low-energy flat screens has also saved energy, along with installing electronic timers for all water heating and cooling units and coffee machines. These ensure that the equipment only operates during working hours.

Manchester Rusk has also reduced the amount of water it uses by installing technologies such as water-efficient toilets.

Production processes

The company invested in new machinery for production and packing, which resulted in significant increases in energy efficiency. It is, on average, 38 per cent more efficient than the old machinery and has increased productivity: the packing line, which used to fill 30 sachets per minute, can now fill 90 in the same time period – an increase of 200 per cent.

Water is an important raw ingredient at Manchester Rusk. The company has installed reduction technologies, such as automatic dosage meters, to ensure that its manufacturing processes use only the amount of water needed. Water usage is also monitored by the use of meters that are calibrated at regular intervals.

Two air source heat recovery units in the roof space above the production floor extract excess heat produced by the machinery. These units heat the water required for the production process, avoiding the need to fire boilers specifically for this process.

Air source heat pumps

Air source heat pumps extract heat from the air. A refrigerant (the same as is used to keep your refrigerator cool) absorbs the heat, and then goes through a heat exchanger which transfers the heat from the refrigerant into a useful form:

- air-to-air heat pumps use this heat to provide warm air, which can be circulated to heat premises;
- air-to-water heat pumps, like the ones at Manchester Rusk, use this heat for water which can be utilised in production processes or pumped back into a heating system with radiators or underfloor pipes.

Air source heat pumps are one of many renewable technologies that a business can employ to reduce its carbon emissions and fuel bills.

Transport

Manchester Rusk used to have its own fleet of vehicles to make deliveries. These vehicles have been taken off the road, and now one large vehicle comes once a day to take everything to a central hub from which products are dispatched to customers. This has reduced fuel consumption by 50 per cent, equivalent to around 2,500 litres per year. The company also offers a discount when products are bought in bulk, to encourage a lower number of deliveries.

Furthermore, as a result of the company's efforts to reduce the amount of waste it produces (see below), waste-collection vehicle movement to and from the site has been reduced by 75 per cent.

REDUCING WASTE

Landfill

Once Manchester Rusk increased its energy efficiency, it began to look at the waste it produces. Production manager Dave Wheeler was astounded to find out that his small business was producing 80 tonnes of waste, costing £10,000 per year.

As the company did not have the resources to investigate how this waste could be reduced, it employed Groundwork Manchester to do the legwork. Groundwork's contacts with local waste handlers enabled Manchester Rusk to reduce its waste to landfill by over 90 per cent. The company's investment in this project paid back within ten months.

Manchester Rusk also looked at its wider environmental impact. The company has a policy of using 80 per cent recycled packaging and has trialled 100 per cent recycled packaging. Both use pre-consumer waste; however, Manchester Rusk is also introducing biodegradable packaging, which will decompose within nine months in consumers' compost heaps.

Recently, an old container that could not be recycled was sunk in the factory grounds to create a pond. The company is hoping to develop this into a nature area with vegetation and trees, creating a 'carbon sink'.

Carbon sinks
Plants and trees absorb carbon dioxide from the atmosphere and then store the carbon and release oxygen through a process

called photosynthesis. Planting more trees is therefore considered a form of carbon offsetting. More information on carbon offsetting can be found in Chapter 2.

Organic matter

Dave was still worried, though, about the waste that could not be recycled. As Manchester Rusk is a food manufacturer, this was mostly organic waste left over from the production processes. Legislation prevents such waste being used as animal fodder and it cannot be recycled.

It was a stroke of luck, therefore, when Dave went to a seminar and met Robert Orr, a director of HiRAD Ltd, which turns organic waste into biogas for generating energy renewably. HiRAD was setting up a biogas power plant in Banbury and needed to source organic waste. The waste left over from production processes at Manchester Rusk is ideal for this purpose as it is high in sugar. Now, all organic waste produced at Manchester Rusk, including by-products of production, grass cuttings and food waste from staff meals, goes into an organic container which is collected once a month and taken to the biogas plant. Manchester Rusk also buys back green electricity from the biogas plant, thereby further reducing its environmental impact.

Biogas

During the decomposition of organic matter, when the oxygen supply is cut off, biogas is produced. Biogas is a gas primarily comprised of methane and carbon dioxide. After it is treated to remove corrosive by-products such as hydrogen sulphide, biogas can be stored or used immediately for electricity production, cooking, space heating or water heating. With further treatment it can also be used as fuel for vehicles or distributed through the gas network.

A biogas plant is an anaerobic digester. 'Anaerobic' refers to the absence of oxygen; while 'digester' refers to the bacteria added to breakdown the organic waste. The result is biogas which is burned to produce electricity.

INCENTIVISING STAFF

Although Dave emphasises that 'you can never say you've done enough, you've always got to explore further possibilities', he believes that the greatest benefit of all the changes is that staff at Manchester Rusk can go home at night knowing that they have done as much as they can to improve their environmental performance.

The management at Manchester Rusk is aware that the environmental improvements they have made could not have happened without employee involvement. Staff members were very supportive from day one, and many of them have taken ideas home, such as recycling. Employees are also encouraged to utilise on-site recycling facilities for waste that they cannot recycle at home.

Being involved in the changes has given employees a renewed sense of responsibility. They have also benefited from greater job security that comes from working for a successful company – indeed, as a result of the improvements made, seven new jobs have been created at the firm.

PROMOTING GREEN CREDENTIALS

The environmental improvements made at Manchester Rusk have led to lots of positive publicity for the firm – the company has won three environmental awards and two manufacturing awards. Invitations for guest speakers from the company have provided numerous opportunities for networking and raised the profile of the business. Representatives of the company have also been invited to talk to MPs regarding waste reduction in the food industry and were also interviewed on Manchester radio.

Clients have been very impressed – so much so that a number of customers have asked for help in reducing the environmental impact of their own firms.

OTHER BENEFITS

Cost savings

Furthermore, the changes implemented have helped to save the company 'lots of money very easily'. It would be difficult to think of other measures that could have improved the profitability of the company with such low payback periods.

The positive publicity that the firm has received has also led to further financial support. For example, the North West Food Federation pledged to help with other environmental capital investments that the company intends to makes.

Greater customer base

Before the environmental improvements were undertaken, Manchester Rusk's prospects were limited in terms of market areas. The savings and investment involved in this programme of work have allowed the company to diversify and enter into different markets.

Having environmental credentials in place has recently become a requirement of many tenders and this has enabled Manchester Rusk to take advantage of business opportunities which might otherwise have been missed.

Greater production output means that the company has also secured major contracts with high-profile retailers to supply products on demand.

LESSONS LEARNED

Partnership working

Manchester Rusk believes that the key to success is working in partnership with local support agencies like Groundwork. Although the environmental changes could have been made without this support, 'it would have taken three times longer'.

Relative ease of environmental improvements

Production manager Dave Wheeler says he wishes he had made other businesses more aware of the changes he was making from day one, because they have been a lot easier to implement than expected. Everything that has been done at Manchester Rusk could be replicated by any business in any industry. He says, 'Just do it. When I first started, I thought, "this is going to be a massive, difficult, frustrating project" – but it's been so easy to do. Don't sit around thinking about it, get to it; the benefits are massive.'

Chapter 4

Getting the team on board

We have emphasised the benefits of getting all your staff involved in your efforts to green your business. This chapter will give you some ideas on how to ensure they are with you at the start of the process and how to maintain their enthusiasm and engagement once the initial excitement wears off.

WHY DO YOU NEED THE TEAM ON BOARD?

Your efforts to green your business will only be completely successful if your whole team is on board. Here are a few of the reasons why . . .

You want people to act on your ideas

Many of the low-cost ways in which you can green your business will involve people developing new, less wasteful working habits. To achieve the improvements you know exist, it's important for people to be willing to change.

You want them to have ideas of their own

Why should you do all the hard work? There will be others in your team who, with the right incentives, will be able to come up with some great ideas to help make your business more environmentally-friendly.

You want them to tell your customers what you are doing

As highlighted in previous chapters, going green can be a good news story that increases existing customer loyalty and perhaps attracts new customers. But that won't happen unless people know what you are doing and believe that the change is genuine. A statement of your policy and action plan on your website will take you some of the way, but it will be nowhere near as powerful as people hearing genuine commitment and enthusiasm for the process from people who work with you.

Greening your business can be a motivator for the whole team

Involving the whole team could have wider-reaching benefits for you, too. Many people are concerned about the environment and want to reduce their impact, but often individuals aren't sure what they can do. Being part of a team that is making their work as environmentally friendly as possible, is likely to provide a general boost to the motivation of everyone. The end result could well be a more committed and motivated workforce.

ENTHUSING PEOPLE AND GETTING THEM INVOLVED

There are many things you can do to ensure your team are with you as you green your business. In essence, it's no different from making sure that you are getting the best from them in any other aspect of what they do: senior management should lead by example; make sure that people have ownership of the actions that they will be taking; give people the tools and resources they need to take the actions expected; recognise the effort that people are making and reward their successes; and, finally, be open to changing the plan of action if it is not working.

Here are some ideas on how to get the process right – and make the whole thing more fun.

Gain and demonstrate top-level commitment

Senior managers should be seen to be committed to greening the business, both in what they say and do. The Carbon Trust conducted a survey on employee attitudes to green businesses. It showed that attitudes are positive, but that leadership is essential and bosses should lead by example. A whopping 70 per cent of those surveyed said they wanted to cut carbon emissions, but lacked sufficient leadership. It is no use asking employees to stick to green procedures if the boss is leaving lights on and using disposable plastic cups. For the system to succeed, all players must be on board and management commitment is crucial.

How can you make sure this happens? It's important to convince the relevant people that this is something they need – and want – to do.

Why are you reading this book? Why do you think that action is needed? Can you use the same arguments to persuade others?

You will know best what is likely to persuade each member of your senior team. Work with this knowledge: have the facts and figures on efficiency and cost savings to hand when talking to the person who worries about the money involved; discuss team morale with your staff manager; stress the potential for attracting new customers to people who are involved in expanding the business; and if anyone is a bit of a pessimist, remember to highlight the risks of not making the change. Don't forget to mention doing your bit to save the planet: all but the most sceptical will enjoy feeling that they are doing the right thing, once they are convinced that it is also the sensible thing to do. Chapter 1 should give you many of the arguments you need.

Help
- Information on the Carbon Trust survey on employees' attitudes can be found at: www.thecarbontrust.co.uk

Explain to everyone why you want to change things
Enthusing everyone in your team starts with the same process. You are going to be asking people to make some changes in the way they do things. Even if these changes are really small – like switching off the monitor on their PC when they have a coffee break – people are more likely to start changing, and to keep doing it until the new way becomes a habit, if they can see why they are doing it.

You are also going to be asking everyone to come up with their own ideas on the sorts of changes that you can make: this process will be more productive and more successful if everyone understands exactly what they are trying to achieve.

This is where the overall aim of your environmental policy statement can be useful. If you don't already have one that you are happy with, develop one and get the top team to sign up to it before you start letting the rest of the team know what your aim is. (Of course, if you are reading this because your staff are encouraging you to green the business, you could get them involved in developing the aim itself.) Chapters 2 and 3 give you some guidance on developing an environmental policy.

Involve everyone in working out what to do

Once people understand what you are trying to achieve, it is important to involve them in working out exactly what you are going to do. People are far more likely to do something if they've thought of it themselves, individually or as part of a group, than if they are asked to realise someone else's ideas.

So, once you have expressed the aim of greening the business in a way that is relevant to you, what next? Why not ask everyone what they think needs to change to make the business greener?

You can begin the process by talking about what your own walk-through or environmental check has uncovered. Equally, you may decide it's better to talk to the team before doing this.

Each individual will have their own priorities when it comes to the environment: some will be concerned about tackling climate change; others will be keen on recycling. If you can develop a set of objectives that at the same time contribute to achieving your overall aim of greening the business and also have a positive impact in the specific areas that matter to your team, then you are well on the way to getting everyone to take the actions needed.

And what about those actions? Ask the whole team to come up with suggestions. You could run a brainstorm session at your annual away-day. Or encourage people to get together in small groups and work out what they themselves could do.

Do this, and you will hopefully have a useful list of changes that could be made. Then what? The next step is to develop an action plan, as described in Chapter 2. Obviously, you don't want every little detail being discussed by everyone, or you will never get anywhere. So someone (or a small team of people) will need to translate the mass of ideas into an action plan. The important thing here is to make sure that everyone knows that their ideas were valued, even if they don't make it into the plan. Give people feedback and explain why you chose the actions you did; also let them know what will happen to the ideas that didn't make it this time around. Will you revisit them at a later date; do you want the person who suggested the idea to develop it a bit further?

Do you have a sceptic or two in your midst? With the arsenal of reasons to support the plans you have already developed, you should be able to find something to interest and engage most people. Try your best to get everyone working with you, but if there's still someone who is quite negative, then let them be: the workplace will change around them and they will eventually have to choose whether to go with the flow or find an organisation more suited to their preferred ways of working.

But what if the sceptic is also a disruptive force, putting a downer on your best efforts to engage everyone? You've several options here, including bringing in an external facilitator who can skilfully push the debate onwards while acknowledging their objections, or simply offering them the option not to get involved.

Enable people to make changes

You've got everyone on board and they are keen to start greening the business. It's now crucial that something positive happens.

When you develop your action plan, make sure it includes some 'quick wins': actions that are easy to implement and that will show positive results pretty quickly. This will demonstrate to people that your plans are achievable and will help to keep them enthused. Early results might even convince some of the doubters.

Be realistic about what you are asking people to do. If it takes time, then allow them time to adjust. Don't demand that the office manager instantly switches from your usual paper to a recycled option. Unless a little time (and it will only be a little) is taken to choose the right brand and quality, the change will end up either costing you more or producing the poorer quality paper that put some of your people off making the change in the first place.

If you are asking people to do something they've not done before, make sure they know how to do it. This might sound obvious, but there's simply no point asking people to print on both sides of the paper if you don't show them where the relevant setting is in their software – if you leave it to them to work it out, you'll simply end up with frustrated people who will begin to think that the whole thing is too much hassle to bother with.

If money is required, be prepared to invest. Don't ask people to print double-sided on a printer that requires manual turning over of the pages or that regularly chews up paper when it's passed through for the second side. Buy a new printer that's up to the job: if it's not time to invest in a new printer, delay the change to double-siding until the time is right and, in the meantime, ask people to use the blank side of sheets they've finished with as rough paper.

Keep up to date with government incentives for greener working. For example, at the time of writing, the government operates a salary sacrifice scheme for bicycle purchase, enabling firms to offer bikes at a cost to the employee some 30 to 40 per cent less than the usual retail price.

Don't tell anyone we told you, but sometimes it's OK to cheat! If your team is a bit reluctant to use recycled paper, because they think the end result will be of lower quality, why don't you simply buy some and put it in the printer, then wait to see what happens. Odds are that people won't notice the difference and you can then let them in on the secret. But be careful: this only works on people who can see the funny side of being hoodwinked.

Reminders

An easy way to change habits and encourage staff to be green is to put up posters and stickers to act as reminders. For example, you could hang up a poster in the kitchen reminding staff to only boil the necessary amount of water for hot drinks. Stickers could be also be strategically placed to remind staff to turn out lights when leaving rooms and turn off computers after use.

Help

■ Posters and stickers can be obtained from the Carbon Trust: www.carbontrust.co.uk. Go to the 'start saving' section and then select 'staff awareness posters'.

Tell them how it's going

You have convinced your team to make some changes by showing them that there are benefits for the environment and for the company. They need to know whether their actions are having the results that you were hoping for.

Part of your action plan will be a method for monitoring the impact of the changes you are making. Use this information to keep people up to date with what they have achieved. When they see that small changes they have made are having the desired effect, they will be more motivated to maintain the change and also possibly to try something a little more ambitious.

Some of the ways you can provide feedback to incentivise staff are described later in this chapter, under 'Making it more fun'. You will doubtless have other ideas that will work in your company. However, remember to follow the general rule that success should be celebrated with everyone and problems kept as much as possible with the people who can do something to overcome them. Of course, you should report to everyone if you are not meeting your targets, but better to tell them when you at least have some solutions to offer.

Be willing to change your approach

When you have taken stock of your progress and told everyone how you are doing, it may be time to consider changing part (or indeed all) of your approach. Some things may not be working as well as you had hoped. Is there anything you can do about this? Ask the people involved why they think it's not working well, and see if they have any suggestions for solutions. Be willing to listen to what they have to say, rather than simply insisting they try harder.

On a broader level, why don't you make a point of asking new members of staff what they think of your plans and activities. They will at the very least offer a new perspective; they may also bring with them some useful new ideas based on their experiences of working in a different company.

MAKING IT MORE FUN: IDEAS FOR INCENTIVES

Any process of change can be difficult for people. It is a good idea therefore to make it as much fun as possible. Here, we discuss a number stickers themselves acted as a reminder and, once an individual received a set number of green stickers, they also found a small treat on their desktop. So, you could decide that three green stickers are rewarded by a mini bar of organic Fairtrade chocolate, or something similar. It's very simple, and not at all expensive, but it makes people realise that you are noticing the effort they are putting in, and are grateful for it.

You could step this up a little. Set targets for improvement in, say, the amount of waste that is recycled over a quarter. Any team that achieves or exceeds its target is entitled to a team lunch out, on the company.

If you are looking to make significant changes, consider financial rewards for the key people involved. Maybe you already offer bonuses for people who achieve certain performance targets. Are there aspects of greening your business that you could include within this type of reward system?

Tangible feedback

We have stressed the importance of letting people know about the progress that you have achieved. Making this feedback tangible is a great way of keeping employees enthusiastic about reaching green goals. This simply means using something that illustrates an idea, for example a chart that shows how you are progressing.

You could create a 'thermometer' display to chart how well you are progressing to a goal, like the ones you see outside churches raising funds for a new roof.

Have you considered setting up a 'greening the business' notice board? This could include visual displays of progress alongside calls for new ideas, reminders about what people are meant to be doing, and the announcement of the winners of any recent competitions you have run.

Celebrate!

People like to celebrate and it's a great way to keep up momentum.

Do it when you reach your goal (or, if it is a long-term one, when you meet a milestone along the way). Take ten minutes at the end of a day to share a bottle of bubbly to mark the achievement, or buy a big cake to have with the afternoon cup of tea.

You could also join up with others who are also greening their activities, to celebrate and promote a particular change. Earth Day

of incentives you could use to increase your team's enth
taking on the challenge you are setting them. You will have
of your own and, of course, you will also want to consult yo
see what they would most enjoy.

Competitions and awards

A little friendly competition can work wonders in generating
to problems and in maintaining enthusiasm.

Consider offering a prize for the best idea that will con
greening the business. What about a wind-up torch or a sola
iPod charger as the prize (a quick search of the internet will fir
of appropriate environmental products)? If you set the rules
could encourage people to tell you not only what changes coul
but also how best to make them.

You could also make the implementation of changes into
competition. To encourage people to turn off their computers
how about monitoring how many people actually do it each i
week (or once a week for a month, if that works better for you
prize for the team (or individual) that has the highest 'score' in
the number of times they had remembered to switch off for the

Do you have an 'employee of the month' or similar scheme?
have a 'green employee of the month' award?

Rewards

If you reward the people who help you to green your business
not only encourage them to carry on doing so, but inspire
follow in their footsteps. These rewards do not have to cost yo
money (or indeed anything at all), although you might decide
out a little if the changes are saving you money as well as gree
business.

A simple thank you may be all the reward that is needed. But
other options that add a little fun . . .

As an example, let's think again about the need for people to
their PCs overnight. Could you – or your environmental champ
up a series of unannounced checks on whether people have
done it? One local authority linked this to fixing 'traffic light' st
the machines: green if you had turned it off, red if you had i

(http://ww2.earthday.net/) and National Bike Week (www.bikeweek.org.uk) are just two examples. Often there are local events organised in conjunction with these celebrations, and you may be able to get your team involved. Talk to your local authority or the local branch of a green group such as Friends of the Earth, who should be able to tell you what is going on.

WHAT YOU CAN DO NOW

There are elements of each stage of the process that you can implement straight away and, of course, you should start making it fun right from the word go.

First of all, be sure that you are clear about why you want to green your business, and that you can explain the reasons to other people.

> ### Example
> You have a number of local authorities that are major clients and you know they want to use contractors that are serious about sustainability. Do you have examples of invitations to tender for work that include questions about sustainability? Do you have feedback on contracts that you did not get which includes negative comments relating to your organisation's lack of attention to this area? If you do, use them to support your arguments. Can you also point to other existing or potential customer groups who are likely to be interested in how green you are?

Then persuade members of the senior management team to join you and to demonstrate their leadership in this area through their actions.

> ### Example
> Can you grab a 10-minute slot at a senior management meeting? If you can, offer the managers a menu of actions they can take (leaving the car at home one day per week;

remembering to switch off their PC when in meetings; agreeing to invest a small amount of money in a new, efficient printer) and ask that each of them signs up to one thing. Agree with them that you will be able to track their progress and report on it to the rest of the team.

It should not then take too much effort to set up an initial brainstorming session to gather people's ideas on the changes they can make. When you have done this, you can swiftly move to implementing a few of the 'easy wins', checking on how people are doing (and handing out the chocolate) and then giving everyone some feedback on what has been achieved.

Example

One of the team has noticed that no one turns off the task lamp on their workstation when they go for a tea-break or for lunch. Use volunteers to check the building during the lunch hour and put a green sticker on each lamp that is off. Make a note of who has turned off their lamp each day. Do this every day for a week and then, at the end of the week, call a team meeting. Tell everyone how many green stickers were 'earned' in total and give everyone who received four or more stickers a chocolate (or give the team with the most stickers a small kitty to take to the pub that evening).

THINKING LONGER TERM

Motivating the team in the longer term is about embedding green working into everyday practices, so that they are not an effort, and integrating sustainability into training and performance review.

Green working culture

Embedding green working into the culture of your company will take time. Keep offering incentives and check that senior managers carry on demonstrating their commitment.

Aim to gradually improve both the set-up of the office and the equipment so that, over time, they fully support green working. There's more information on purchasing equipment in Chapter 2 and on refurbishing your premises in Chapter 7.

When things get busy one of the easiest things to drop is often the green scheme. No one has time to walk to work let alone update the notice board with new ideas. Don't beat yourself up if other things take priority. No one is perfect and, so long as you pick up the initiative again when it is more appropriate, you shouldn't feel guilty about the delay in your efforts.

Training

Making green working part of everyday business means including relevant information in your training and development.

Do you include your green goals and targets, and how individuals are expected to contribute towards them, as part of your induction process for new staff?

Why not encourage your facilities manager to improve their expertise in energy management? Or perhaps in wider environmental management?

Help

- The Energy Institute run a series of short courses that will equip people with basic energy management skills. More information can be found at: www.energyinst.org.uk (click on 'education and training' and then look at the current list of short courses).
- The Institute for Environmental Management and Assessment offers a range of information and training on environmental management. See www.iema.net and click on 'training'.

Have you thought about increasing everyone's understanding of environmental issues and the role that they can play? Greater understanding can increase motivation. You could theme an away-day around the environment and bring in some experts to talk about the issues and run workshops to encourage people to think about what more you can do, both as a business and as individuals.

Performance review

There is probably a system in place in your company to review each individual's performance in their role. It will likely cover a lot of different areas such as technical competence, the way they deal with your customers and their general behaviour.

In the long term, if you want green ways of working to be a part of the company's identity, these should somehow be included in this system. Exactly how they are included will depend on the business you are in and on the job of that particular person. For some organisations, it will be about knowing what the latest energy-saving devices are and whether they are sufficiently cost effective for you to invest in; for others it may be a more general part of the overall behaviours that you expect them to follow when in the workplace.

TAKE THE FIRST STEP

It's time to put down the book again, and do something.

Write down why you want to green your business. Then take those arguments and use them to convince just one of your senior colleagues to join you. Then, together, you can take the proposal to the whole senior management team.

Now you are ready to get the whole team on board. If you have an away-day coming up, book a slot for an ideas brainstorming session. A few days before the away-day, explain your ideas to the team at a staff meeting and warn them that you will be asking for input at the away-day. On the day itself, collect the ideas for action and then ask everyone to vote for their favourite. Give a small prize to the person who suggested it, and secure everyone's commitment to implementing it when you get back to work the following day.

ACTION CHECKLIST

Things to do now	Done
Be clear about why you want to green the business	
Convince the senior management team to join you	
Explain to the whole team what you are trying to do	
Organise a session where everyone contributes their ideas	

Try a few simple changes and give everyone feedback	
Set up one or two simple incentive schemes	
Things to do after this	**Done**
Incorporate greening the business into your induction process	
Have someone trained in energy and/or environmental management	
Organise a 'green' away-day for the team	
Revisit your aims: are the senior team still actively committed?	

RECOMMENDED LINKS

For more general information on motivating your team through any process of change, visit the Business Link website: www.businesslink.gov.uk (click on 'employing people' and look for the section on 'motivation').

The Carbon Trust has a series of awareness-raising resources that are available for free. For more information, go to www.thecarbontrust.co.uk (click on 'solutions' and look for 'order posters . . .' within the SME business toolkit box).

For training courses, check out the Institute for Environmental Management and Assessment (www.iema.net) and the Energy Institute (www.energyinst.org.uk).

Chapter 5

Promoting your company's green credentials

In previous chapters we've discussed both short- and long-term actions you can implement to make your business more sustainable. Here we show why and how you can successfully promote your company's green credentials and what benefits your business can reap as a consequence.

WHY PROMOTE YOUR GREEN CREDENTIALS?

If you have acted on some of the recommendations made in previous chapters, the next step is to let people know. Promoting your green image can improve your reputation and give you a competitive edge over other organisations, as well as motivate your workforce.

Demonstrating your commitment to sustainable development can be creative, satisfying and profitable. This chapter is not intended to provide basic marketing advice; it is assumed that most companies will already have marketing plans in place. But you'll find ideas on how to use your green credentials to attract and retain customers while ensuring that your marketing strategy has a minimal impact on the environment. For more information and tips on marketing, refer to the *Good Small Business Guide*, which is part of this series of books.

Meet customer demand

More and more customers want to know how a business is managed and the impacts, both positive and negative, on the environment. Smart marketing of your community and environmental achievements can help to create customer loyalty. A recent study conducted by Search Futures Observatory found that up to 73 per cent of consumers rank a brand's environmental attributes as the third most important factor when making a purchase.

Win new customers

Promoting your green credentials can also help you win new customers who are looking to buy from ethical and sustainable companies. Lots of small and medium-sized enterprises compete against large organisations. Using your eco-credentials to differentiate yourself from your competitors can give your business the edge.

Gaining this competitive edge requires effective and astute promotion and marketing. It is essential that your employees, stakeholders and customers know about your responsible business practices.

In Chapter 4, we looked at nationally and internationally recognised accreditation such as EMAS or ISO 14001. A number of organisations, especially those in the public sector, have procurement strategies that require suppliers and contractors to hold a particular level of environmental accreditation. If, after conducting your environmental check you choose to obtain an environmental accreditation, make sure you publicise it.

Keep staff motivated

As mentioned in previous chapters, promoting your green credentials and ensuring that staff are aware of the ethos of the business, including its aims and objectives, will also help boost staff morale, retain staff and encourage new recruits. Get your employees involved in the process and encourage them to market your green credentials.

Attract investors

Sustainability has become an established concept; you only have to open a newspaper to see articles dedicated to green issues. Although financial bodies are predicting that the economy will continue to slow down over the next few years, in the field of sustainable development and climate change there is still significant potential for growth.

The business sector has welcomed the commercial opportunities that sustainability offers. John Willman, UK business editor at the Financial Times, suggests that 'Anything relating to climate change [has the potential for growth because] people are convinced of the importance of reducing carbon emissions and want to do something about it.' By promoting your green credentials, you will increase your chances of cropping up on the radar of investors who are looking to back this market and businesses are more likely to think of your organisation as a good investment opportunity.

WHAT YOU CAN DO TO PROMOTE YOUR CREDENTIALS

Messages to use

The first step is to embed your policies, actions and general sustainability messages in all communication, both internal and external. One of the easiest ways of doing this is to develop a sustainability mission statement. This sets out your business objectives in a short and concise document. You could either develop a separate mission statement that covers environmental sustainability, or you could incorporate your green principles into an existing mission statement. Ideally, being a green business shouldn't be a separate part of your business's identity, but integrated into every aspect of your business operations. For more information about mission statements, see the boxes below.

Mission statements

Typically a mission statement should include three elements:

1 the purpose statement, which specifies what the company is trying to achieve;
2 the business statement, which outlines the activities or programmes of work that will enable the company to meet the purpose; and
3 the values statement.

Unless your company is specifically offering environmentally-sustainable products and services, your values statement should reflect your green credentials. The values are the beliefs that the company's members hold in common and try to put into practice.

The MacMillan Academy mission statement

The MacMillan Academy is a school for children in years 7 to 11 which has a special focus on science and outdoor education. It also offers a number of courses for older children. The Academy redrafted its mission statement in September 2006 to incorporate their commitment to sustainability.

'We wish to keep environmental issues as a priority. We also support a wider sustainability agenda. Students will be encouraged to understand the personal, local, national and international implications of not doing so.'

The Co-operative Bank mission statement

The Co-operative Bank demonstrates through its mission statement that it is possible to incorporate the value of sustainability into both the purpose and business statements.

'We, The Co-operative Bank, will continue to develop our business, taking into account the impact our activities have on the environment and society at large. The nature of our activities are

> *such that our indirect impact, by being selective in terms of the provision of finance and banking arrangements, is more ecologically significant than the direct impact of our trading operations.'*
>
> The statement goes on to indicate that not only will the bank pursue its own objectives, but they will also strive to help and encourage all its partners to do likewise.

You should include information on the green projects and activities you are doing as well as what you have already achieved. For example, if you have attained an environmental standard, reduced your carbon emissions, or changed your procurement policies to take into account sustainability issues, then let people know.

Here are some ideas of the types of initiatives you could promote.

Achievements

What achievements have you made already? Include facts and figures such as how much:

- you have cut your carbon footprint;
- money you have saved by 'going green';
- you have reduced your waste;
- your water consumption has reduced.

If you have won any environmental awards or received recognition for sustainability, then shout about them.

Case study

In April 2008 Bosinver Farm Cottages became certified through the Green Tourism Business Scheme (www.greenbusiness.co.uk). The certification process looks at 120 different measures over seven categories:

- energy
- water

- purchasing
- waste
- transport
- natural and cultural heritage
- innovation

The cottages were awarded Gold, the highest standard available, and now display the scheme's symbol at the top of their website. This links to a web page which is dedicated to the awards they have won as a business and the environmental achievements made. It is also an opportunity for the owners to describe why preserving the environment is important to them and to suggest a few ways that their customers can be more sustainable tourists.

Plans

If you're still at the planning stage, this doesn't have to stop you from promoting yourself as a green company. Let people know about the targets you are working on, such as:

- how much you plan to cut your carbon emissions, or when you hope to be carbon neutral;
- how you plan to spend the money that you'll save by going green.

Making your business greener is a continuous process. So once you've started promoting the goals you've already achieved, make sure you promote your new ones as well.

Methods

Include interesting snippets of information about how you made these achievements, such as:

- how you've engaged staff about the issue;
- interesting or unusual ideas that staff have had;
- comments from staff who have changed their travel arrangements, e.g. walking or cycling to work rather than using the car.

Case study

SweatyBetty started as a single shop selling women's active wear in 1997. It has since grown into a national chain and website retailer with an ethical stance. Its website includes a page of achievements, from eliminating photocopiers to its stringent suppliers manual, and also illustrates its policy on cycling to work.

'We know that cycling to work not only helps to save the planet but also gives you a pert bum! So we contribute £50 towards every new bicycle that our Betties buy to travel to work. Can you believe 50% of our support office staff come to work on two wheels or on foot? Only 20% – drive a car but we know who they are and where they live!'

Engage with your customers

Many firms have successfully used the environment as a topic on which they can engage with their customers. For example, adding some general facts and figures to communications about environmental achievements can increase interest.

Case study

The clothing firm Howies prides itself on its environmental credentials. There is a prominent page on its website (under 'environment') with the heading: 'Too busy sipping latte to save the rainforest'. The page outlines the company's view that we are not dealing with the environmental problems we have created. The statement ends with the line: '12,090 trees were cut down in the time it took to read this'.

Your mission statement can also put your achievements in context and illustrate why you are doing additional work to make your business greener.

Case study

Innocent Drinks has a Web page dedicated to resource efficiency. The company has started work on reducing its carbon footprint and lets its customers know by showing how many grams of carbon dioxide are produced for every bottle of smoothie it sells. As these numbers can be meaningless on their own, this section of the website begins:

'If everyone lived as we do in the UK we would need three planets to support us. Problem is we only have one available, and the resources on this one are either in a state of decline or simply running out.'

Selling your environmental credentials is also an opportunity to get your customers to talk to you. The web-based retailer Pedlars ends its page about the environment with: 'If you'd like to find out more about our attempts to make Pedlars an environmentally-friendly company, or you have a suggestion that might help us to achieve our goals, we'd be delighted to hear from you.'

Your target audience

As with all communications, think about who your audience are.

Communicating internally

We've already discussed how involving your staff in every stage of greening your business will help to boost their motivation. It will also make them more likely to promote your green image to external organisations.

Many of the ideas given in Chapter 4 are ways of promoting your green image to your staff. If you've appointed an environmental champion, they can be the first point of contact for all staff members who want to find out more about the organisation's green credentials, or the person who praises staff for their efforts and achievements. However, it's not enough just to inform staff about achievements and what is working; it's equally important to let them know about areas for improvement.

How about giving regular updates to your staff at team meetings? If your company uses an Intranet, set up pages that give feedback on what the company is doing to reduce its impact on the environment and the progress made. If you want to give information about a particular topic or issue, set aside half an hour or an hour for a presentation. Ad hoc e-mails to staff when something new arises are also a good idea.

Communicating with staff

Squiz is a software development group, based in New Zealand and Australia, that is committed to reducing its carbon footprint. It has taken a novel approach to reduce the number of computers left on overnight by developing a text system which alerts staff if their workstations are left on after business hours. This system encourages staff to shut down computers, thereby saving electricity and reducing carbon emissions.

Communicating externally

Outside of your business, there are three groups of people to whom you should communicate your green credentials:

- existing customers;
- potential customers;
- investors (including partner organisations and other stakeholders).

Before you start promoting your green credentials, be clear about what you want to achieve. For example, are you trying to communicate the benefits of a product or service, or are you trying to persuade potential clients to switch brands.

Existing customers

Start communicating with your existing customers straight away. One of the easiest ways of doing this is by e-mail. Why not include a message at the bottom which demonstrates the business's eco-credentials, for example how much carbon dioxide you have saved in the last month/quarter/year? You can create a set of different e-mail signatures to allow you to vary the message ending.

If you are able to put pre-recorded messages on your phone system, instead of playing 'Greensleeves' to people on hold, have a recording of your mission statement.

There are also interactive ways of getting your message across. Rather than sending a generic Christmas card, how about donating to an environmental charity or project? You could even get your clients to choose by asking them to vote from a list of charities. For example, Impetus Consulting Ltd decided to send an electronic card to its clients and partners which allowed recipients to vote from a choice of three charities. The charity with the most votes received a £500 donation.

A designated environmental champion can also act as a focal point for clients who want to know more about the organisation's social and environmental achievements.

Potential customers

Incorporating messages and news about your green image in existing marketing channels is one of the quickest ways to promote your credentials. The Internet is not only a good vehicle for selling your services, but also a perfect window for customers to view the profile of your business. If you produce flyers, newsletters, or other publications, be certain to include information about your mission statement and any achievements or activities.

Reeds Printers

Reeds Printers, a member of the Cumbria Green Business Forum, is a printing business in the North of England. The company produces a range of items, from small stationery products to full-colour magazines and books, and draw tickets to fine art reproductions.

The organisation endeavours to act in an environmentally-friendly manner in terms of its direct – and indirect – actions on the environment. The company's green credentials are publicised on its website, where copies of its environmental policy are available to download.

The website (www.reeds-printers.co.uk) highlights the awards that Reeds Printers have won (including ISO 14001 certification and the Cumbria Environmental Network Gold Award status) as well as the company's ambitions (e.g. to hold on to the ISO 14001 certification and achieve Forestry Stewardship Council status). The website also highlights some of the company's key practices, e.g. selecting recycled and environmentally-friendly materials and operating a 'cycle to work' scheme.

Networking is a good face-to-face method of publicising your eco-credentials while building new business contacts. There are a number of events that combine both business networking and sustainability, e.g. Sponge, a network for young professionals with an interest in sustainable development and the built environment (www.spongenet.org) and the Energy Institute (www.energyinst.org.uk), as well as various locally based networks such as Hampshire's Sustainable Business Network (www.the-sbp.co.uk).

Investors

Investors, including partner organisations, are likely to require evidence that your organisation practises what it preaches. But, other than information about your existing green credentials, the majority of actions related to engaging with your investors will take place over the longer term.

THINKING LONGER TERM

One way of looking at marketing and promotion in the longer term is to develop a marketing strategy. This doesn't mean you have to produce a long, drawn-out document. An effective strategy simply needs to explain how you are going to sell and promote the vision of your business. For some small and medium-sized businesses a one-page document that everyone can easily read is often the best approach.

Messages to use

In the short term, communicating your mission statement and achievements is vital. However, for longer-term planning you should develop specific messages for different audiences.

All the people you need to communicate with (staff, new and existing customers and investors) will have different reasons for wanting to know about your green image and for choosing to do business with you. So, it's important to understand why green credentials have attracted your existing customers and how publicising your green actions will attract new business.

Staff and investors

Your staff and any partner organisations, such as your suppliers and co-producers, as well as investors, will need to know about your ethos, strategies and policies. Often the key message for this audience is that you practise what you preach.

Customers

Before you can communicate your green credentials to your customers effectively, find out what it is that inspires them to seek out organisations with green credentials.

For example, if your customers are already very engaged in sustainability issues and they take a proactive and whole-hearted approach to living a more ethical and green lifestyle, your message to them is likely to be different from the message to customers who are aware of the issues and feel guilty about their lifestyle (or their organisation's activities) and buy from 'good' companies and boycott 'bad' companies.

The following suggestions apply predominantly to businesses offering products and services to individual consumers (as opposed to other businesses), although business-to-business companies might find some of this information useful, for instance in targeting their marketing at specific individuals within those businesses.

A number of organisations have undertaken research into green consumerism. A good place to start understanding what your clients are looking for is the Green Light tool (see the box below). This tool describes the different consumer groups and provides examples of good marketing.

In some cases, it may be necessary to create a need in your customers. According to the Green Light tool, approximately 35 per cent of the UK population are 'conveniently conscious'. People in this category tend to be aware of, and fairly concerned about, environmental change and ethical issues. They will do things they suppose are 'easy', but are not interested in ethical consumption or local issues. For this group, start small and gradually introduce the idea of your green credentials.

The Green Light tool

'Green isn't just the new black; it's here to stay. But what should brands communicate about their green credentials, how, to whom and where? Green Light brings clarity and offers a framework to inform all stages of the communication planning process.'

Andre McGarrigle, Head of Commercial Planning and Research, Guardian News and Media

The research segmented the UK population into five types of people:

1 onlookers (26%)
2 conveniently conscious (35%)
3 positive choosers (31%)
4 vocal activists (4%)
5 principled pioneers (4%)

The tool provides guidance on how to target the green messages across the different segments. For example, other benefits (rather than sustainability) motivate 'onlookers' and the key messages to get across are the cost-saving ones, i.e. if you choose this product, you will save energy and therefore money. Positive choosers, on the other hand, look for information that will help them to make their choices and demand transparency in the companies they choose to support.

The Green Light tool is in the research section of www.adinfo-guardian.co.uk.

Once you have an idea of the different demographics of your client base, you can create separate messages that target each group.

There are several messages to get across. You want to empower your customers and make them feel that, by using your products or services, they can make a difference. Once again, you will need to demonstrate that you practise what you preach.

How to communicate effectively

Futerra has produced two publications that provide general principles to employ when communicating the climate change message. These are *The Rules of the Game* and *New Rules: New Game.* Some of the principles outlined confront established beliefs about what works, for example 'don't rely on concerns about children's future or human survival instincts'. However, they have been compiled using comprehensive evidence on changing attitudes towards climate change.

You can download the publications from the website: www.futerra.co.uk.

Communicating internally

A longer-term focus of communicating internally is to attract new recruits. Vanessa Robinson, Manager of Organisation and Resourcing at the Chartered Institute of Personnel and Development (CIPD) suggests that, for younger people and those at the beginning of their working life, the credibility of the prospective employer and their social and environmental aspirations may be an important consideration.

In order to encourage these individuals to work for your company, it is vital to incorporate your company's ethos, accreditations and achievements in recruitment literature and ensure that the same messages are incorporated on your website.

Don't forget that your staff are your best sales force. It is important that they have information not only about the company's ethos, but about what is being done on a day-to-day basis to implement this. Your staff are the contact points for your customers and can ensure the green message reaches them.

Communicating externally

Existing customers

Rewarding customer loyalty will help you to retain existing customers.

The following marketing ideas are most relevant for businesses that sell products and services to other businesses, rather than to individuals, although some of the suggestions might also be of benefit to the latter.

You can reward customer loyalty through corporate hospitality, such as entertaining clients at spectator events like sports matches or the theatre. One of the objectives of corporate hospitality is to provide a relaxed atmosphere where you can find out more about the requirements of your clients in order to expand your business contacts and increase sales.

In the same way that your eco-credentials can help differentiate you from your competitors and give you a competitive edge, corporate hospitality can also help set you apart. By combining elements of your green credentials in your corporate hospitality activities (how about choosing an event with a low carbon footprint and using sustainable travel to get there?) you can have an even bigger impact.

You can also reward customer loyalty by treating your customers to lunch or dinner, or inviting them to a party to mark a special occasion. Remember to incorporate sustainability into the mix, for instance by choosing a sustainable venue, buying the food locally and ensuring that the event is easy to get to by public transport.

At events and parties, corporate gifts are sometimes offered to act as a reminder for your customers. You can use this as another way of communicating your green credentials by creating appropriate gifts such as fabric shopping bags with your logo and a green message.

Working with your local community can be a key marketing tool and a means of promoting your green image. We've mentioned separating your target audience into different groups, including 'positive choosers' who demand that the businesses they use are transparent in their operations and practice what they preach. Working with your community is a way of building trust and demonstrating this transparency. Again, there are ways of incorporating sustainability into this work. You could give away your old equipment to community projects, which has a double benefit of helping the community and reducing your waste. You could also give your staff the option to volunteer for a community organisation or project for a few days each year and encourage them to choose opportunities that benefit the environment.

However, a few words of caution regarding communications aimed at retaining existing customers. It's important that your customers are able to believe in the legitimacy of your product and the claims you are making. As more and more companies are jumping on the green bandwagon, potential customers are likely to become more sceptical of any claims made.

You also need to be able to demonstrate to your customers that adhering to a green policy does not compromise your product. Your customers will have to be convinced that your product performs the job it's supposed to – they won't sacrifice product quality just because it will help the environment. In any case, products that don't work are more likely to end up thrown out in the rubbish, which goes against what you are trying to achieve.

Think about your pricing, too. If you're charging a premium for your product – and many environmentally-friendly products cost more, often because they use higher-quality materials – make sure that your customers can afford the premium and feel it's worth it.

Potential customers

Researching who your customers are (as suggested earlier) may highlight a whole group of potential customers you have not yet engaged with. Alternatively, you can specifically seek out a group of customers who require certain aspects of your new green credentials – for example some public sector organisations require external contractors to hold an environmental accreditation. How can they become your new clients? Use these opportunities to target them through your marketing strategy.

One way of communicating your message to potential customers is to use direct marketing. This is marketing aimed at, and distributed directly to, a defined audience. The key to its success is reaching the right people in a cost-effective way. The objectives of direct marketing range from encouraging customers to buy specific products that you are promoting, to reinforcing other forms of communication. Specific objectives of promoting your green image could include:

- raising awareness of your green values;
- generating sales among ethically conscious consumers;
- building relationships with potential partners.

One form of direct marketing that can be very effective is direct mail. However, direct mail is 'junk mail' to many (often most) of its recipients. The box below provides tips for ensuring that you communicate your green credentials via your direct mail campaign, while ensuring that the campaign itself has a minimal impact on the environment.

Other forms of direct marketing include e-mail marketing and telemarketing, both of which are likely to have less of an impact on the environment than direct mail. With e-mail marketing you can tailor your message to your audience, for example highlighting different messages depending on which category your customers fall under (see the Green Light tool, above).

Top tips for green direct marketing

- Use marketing methods that have a lower environmental impact, such as e-mails rather than direct mail marketing.
- Combine e-mail marketing with direct mail marketing to reduce the impact of the latter, e.g. if you usually send out a catalogue by post every month, send it bi-monthly and back it up with e-mails every other month.
- Have a well-maintained database to reduce mailings going out to contacts who have moved on.
- Use your e-mails to give your contacts an easy way to update the contact details you hold for them to help maintain your database.
- Tailor your e-mails to get the most relevant message to the different groups.
- Use environmentally-friendly materials such as recycled paper when promoting your green image.
- Use vegetable-based inks, which are less damaging to the environment and are easier to recycle.

- Pay attention to the type of print finishing, e.g. use water-based coatings as opposed to UV-varnished finishes.
- Think about the print size and format – can you make the marketing materials smaller?
- Make sure it is worth doing – sending out an unnecessary mailing will paint a particularly bad environmental image.
- Consider the shelf-life of printed materials – how quickly will they go out of date? Is there a layout and way of binding that enables you to update the material without a full reprint?
- Remember to measure the success of the campaign to see if it's worth repeating or to find out if there are any lessons you can use.
- Use your imagination – include messages about your green credentials, such as printing snippets about how much energy you have saved on the outside of the envelopes.
- Publicise your actions – if you have taken the actions above, let people know.
- Use the Futerra publications mentioned earlier to ensure you are using the right words to communicate your sustainability message.

There are many 'indirect' ways of communicating messages. Some of these will also have the benefit of producing minimal amount of waste and should therefore get priority in any 'green' marketing campaign. These include the local media – television, radio and newspapers/magazines. Using the local media means you'll reach customers in your area, so people won't have to travel too far to get to you, which will minimise their environmental impact.

Media relations

Think carefully about which publications to incorporate your messages into. Readers of newspapers such as *The Guardian* are more likely to already be on board with the sustainability message than, say, readers of *The Daily Telegraph*.

Internet

You will also need to use the Internet to support and boost your overall marketing message. While an initial marketing push such as an article in the local paper may capture someone's attention, people will turn to the Internet to gather information on additional questions they may have. Although you will need to provide information to back up your product or service, you can take this opportunity to promote your green credentials. Highlight any activities you have undertaken, accreditations you have achieved or awards you have won (see the section below on investors). The Internet is relatively environmentally-friendly because people can choose to print off the information they want as opposed to being bombarded with lots of junk mail they probably won't read.

Internet marketing is also good for products and services that people feel strongly about, and green products often fall into this category. Use online communities to build loyalty by having chat and discussion boards to bring people together to discuss issues of interest. Some online communities focus on green issues, for example www.dothegreenthing.com.

Viral marketing

Viral marketing is essentially word of mouth on the Internet. It works well if it concerns an issue that opinion leaders want to be associated with. Given that green issues are rising up the agenda and people want to be seen to be reducing their environmental impact, viral marketing can be successfully linked to green products and services. However, the benefits must be genuine and apparent because the key to viral marketing is getting people to tell their friends about the product and they will literally be putting their reputation on the line.

Networking

Another way of reaching new customers is by attending networking events. These give you the opportunity to talk to others about your products as well as about your green ethos. Obtaining speaker opportunities at events is another way of boosting your reputation and raising awareness of your environmental values.

Sponsorship

By sponsoring and supporting appropriate local events, you can signal your commitment to the local environment and the community. Depending on the event, it will raise your profile among existing customers, or offer a way of reaching new customers. It will also provide you with good publicity as well as giving you opportunities for public speaking.

Investors

Entering (and winning) sustainability awards is a good way of demonstrating to investors that you are genuinely leading by example. This can also have a number of additional benefits, such as making you focus on your achievements, boosting staff morale and setting you apart from your competition. It can also put you in good stead for other promotional activities such as public speaking opportunities and producing press materials.

Direct Marketing Association Awards

The Direct Marketing Association hosts an annual awards ceremony and in 2007 it introduced a Green Award that recognises environmental best practice. To be in with a chance of winning you need to demonstrate a direct marketing campaign that responds to the awards' key criteria of creativity, strategy and results, as well as evidence of how it has reduced its environmental impact.

No one won the gold award in the first year (as it was felt the industry could still do better), but Greentomatocars (an environmentally-friendly taxi company based in West London) won the silver award for its 'Pass it on' door drop campaign. To reduce the waste associated with a traditional mail drop, the company produced a single door drop for recipients to pass around the neighbourhood. Recipients could tick off their address to show they had seen it and were encouraged to write down the company's number.

Royal Mail won the bronze award by producing the company's customer magazine for senior marketers in blue-chip companies, introducing them to environmentally-friendly print and production methods.

More information about the award is on the website: www.dmaawards.org.uk (under the 'strategy' category).

Once you have got into your stride, consider joining a sustainable business partnership. These are generally informal networks of businesses working in the sustainable development field or in a different area but that act responsibly and incorporate sustainability into their values. A business partnership is a good opportunity to meet like-minded businesses and develop contacts, both in terms of new commercial opportunities and in sharing best practices and raising your company's profile. You can share ideas that have – or haven't – worked and seek advice from those in the same position as you. Sometimes they offer free services to help with sustainable business practices.

West Sussex Sustainable Business Partnership

This is an example of a business partnership with a particular focus on sustainability. It aims to 'motivate and support businesses within West Sussex to adopt sustainable business practices.'

A range of free support and advice is available including:

- resource efficiency training and environmental legislation workshops
- environmental reviews of business premises
- energy audits
- newsletter
- technical helpline

In Chapter 2 we discussed the idea of working with other small businesses as a means of reducing the impact of your company on climate change. Remember to use these networks as a marketing tool to help you develop your customer base and meet potential investors. You can either encourage the members of the networks to become your customers, or you might be able to take advantage of cross-selling opportunities. For example, you might meet a company that offers services complementary to yours and which has already successfully promoted the green message to its customers. See if they will recommend your services to its customers.

TAKE THE FIRST STEP

Gather together your environmental management team and develop a sustainability mission statement, or incorporate your green values into your existing mission statement.

Once you have your mission statement, you can get your environmental champion to spread the word amongst your staff. Give them an update at a team meeting, or send them ad-hoc e-mails highlighting activities that the company has done.

To communicate to existing customers and partners, you could create a series of e-mail signatures that staff can use at the bottom of their e-mails.

And then you can begin to look at how you can green your existing marketing activities.

ACTION CHECKLIST

Things to do now	Done
Create a sustainability mission statement	
Create a page on your Intranet to keep staff informed of green activities and progress	
Highlight any awards, accreditations or achievements on the company website	
Create e-mail signatures to highlight achievements and messages	
Record your mission statement to use as hold music on your phone system	
Incorporate your green messages into existing marketing materials	

Research networking events in your area that have a sustainability focus and attend them	
Read the Futerra publications about general principles for communicating the climate change message	
Things to do after this	**Done**
Read the Green Light tool to find out which categories your customers fall into and why they care whether or not you have green credentials	
Create tailored messages for your different audiences	
Incorporate your company's ethos, accreditations and achievements into your recruitment literature	
Incorporate elements of your green credentials into your next corporate hospitality event	
Research how you can incorporate sustainability into any community work you are doing	
Look at your marketing strategy and analyse the sustainability of it or develop a sustainable marketing strategy	
Enter a sustainability award	
Join a sustainable business partnership	

RECOMMENDED LINKS

For general advice about marketing, including advice on online marketing, visit the 'sales and marketing' section of the Business Link website: www.businesslink.gov.uk.

For research about public attitudes to climate change, visit the Ipsos Mori website www.ipsos-mori.com (click on the 'publications and archive' link at the top and then go to the 'social reports' section).

For advice on communicating the climate change message, download *The Rules of the Game* and *New Rules: New Game* from the Futerra website www.futerra.co.uk.

Use the Green Light tool found in the research section of www.adinfoguardian.co.uk for guidance on how to target the green messages across different audience segments.

Check out the following websites for sustainability events in your area: Sponge (www.spongenet.org) and the Energy Institute (www.energyinst.org.uk).

Case Study 3

Preserving the intrinsic value of the environment

First Impressions Last Longer, which is based in Croydon, South London, was founded in 2004 by Bruce and Yasmin Halai-Carter and is Europe's first carbon neutral company specialising in office supplies. It has been nominated for the Croydon green business of the year no less than five times.

The company has based its business model on the values of sustainability. Right from the start, First Impressions set out to be an environmentally and socially responsible company. It has achieved this with great success and without compromising the viability of the business.

The central aim and vision of the company is to source and supply office supplies that have minimal impact on the environment. In recognition of its commitment to preserving the environment, the company has a mission paper and environmental policy, available on its website, which sets out clear practices and includes measurable targets, such as:

- the recycling rate should fall no lower than 80 per cent;
- waste to landfill will not exceed 1kg per person/month;
- waste to recycling will not exceed 30kg per person/month;
- reused materials – no more than 1000kg of packaging bought per year;
- private car travel no higher than 50 miles per month; and
- public transport no higher than 500 miles per month.

As Yasmin, co-founder of First Impressions, states: 'When we started the company we wanted to create a business whose process had the environment in mind from inception so we would not have to artificially re-engineer the company to become green.'

RESOURCE EFFICIENCY AND CARBON MANAGEMENT

As highlighted above, the company has in place protocols and targets to ensure it operates at maximum efficiency. For example, a recycling target of 80 per cent is included in the company's environmental strategy. Since November 2006, the company has not bought any new packaging. To wrap and package orders, it uses boxes and packaging from goods delivered by manufacturers or collects unwanted packaging from a network of local businesses. In addition, shredded paper produced by the company is used as internal packaging. To date, the company is exceeding this target, with recycling rates at 84 per cent.

To reduce energy consumption the company has taken part in the Envibe Challenge. Launched in 2006, the Envibe Challenge works closely with businesses in Croydon to provide support on how businesses can improve their green credentials. The project includes an accreditation scheme, whereby businesses can work towards bronze, silver and gold status. More information can be found at: www.envibe.co.uk/challenge.html.

In 2007 First Impressions invited Envirowise to conduct a review and discovered that the company was running at less than a third of the recommended good practice in energy efficiency guidelines for gas and within good practice for electricity (which is supplied from renewable sources).

A great deal of time and effort is devoted to developing a bespoke and unique range of environmentally sensitive products. First Impressions works closely with manufacturers to increase the number of products produced entirely from UK post-consumer waste. In addition, the business employs the principle of 'we buy it, we're responsible for it', which means the material carbon cost for every product sold is offset by the company at a rate of 140 per cent. Together, these have helped First Impressions reach its carbon neutral status.

Premises

To its advantage, First Impressions owns its own premises so is able to implement modifications freely. Heat from the server, which is located in the main office, is used to heat the office. Furthermore, the building is well insulated, which eliminates the need for further heating requirements. The company has also decided not to install a hot water boiler and all electricity is from renewable sources.

Partnership working, streamlined production and distribution

The company has intentionally based all of its business operations in the UK. First Impressions deals directly, and has built mutually beneficial working relationships, with manufacturers. This gives the company more control over the whole supply chain – from product to distribution. In fact, when tendering for procurement contracts, First Impressions tender on a co-operative basis with the manufacturers of the required products. Thus, clients are able to see the supply chain in full, and this streamlined approach cuts back on unnecessary administrative costs, further cutting overheads and providing a significant competitive edge over other contactors that are unable to avoid these administration costs.

In addition, Bruce and Yasmin's choice to use only UK-based manufacturers significantly reduces transport costs and virtually eliminates carbon emissions from air freight. Deliveries are made using LPG vans, although the company is currently in discussions with a company developing a battery-operated transit van. For other business transport, the company uses a hybrid car which has provided savings, both carbon and financial.

ENVIRONMENTAL CHECKS

Although the company's environmental policy requires regular detailed internal audits to monitor progress against targets, the company has recently decided to work towards ISO 14002 : 2004, which they hope to achieve in 2008. The company will continue with its in-depth internal auditing process, but ISO accreditation will provide First Impressions with a respected and independent certification.

PROMOTING GREEN ENTERPRISE

First Impressions aims to be transparent in its business operations. The company publishes a monthly report on its environmental performance (available on its website) and each customer invoice includes a statement, highlighting the environmental efficiency of the products bought.

Wider activities include engaging with grassroots environmental campaigns to ensure the company keeps up to date with new developments. As Yasmin explains: 'We put the environment front and centre to everything we do and especially customer and client relations. Our customers come to us because of the reputation we have developed and because they want to do the best that they can. We have secured a number of high-profile contracts on the basis of our unique bespoke way of supply and because we have proved consistently that switching to greener supplies does actually save money long term.'

Demonstrating the benefits of 'going green' to small companies is a bigger challenge, but First Impressions has been very successful especially with companies that are willing to share information about their consumption and really do see the benefits. One way of nudging people in the right direction has been the introduction of the company's Urban Fossil Awards; a series of certificates which acknowledge the sustainable procurement decisions of clients. For existing clients, there is the First Club, which offers tailored support and research on a company's administration and procurement performance.

EMPLOYEE INVOLVEMENT

Being a small business, staff at First Impressions work together closely. The organisation has been praised for its education and training programmes. Staff members are provided with information on the scientific premise of climate change, but in line with the foundations of sustainable development, staff are also able to learn and discuss social issues that arise as a result of environmental problems.

Chapter 6

Adapting your business to climate change

In earlier chapters, we looked at why and how you should reduce carbon emissions from your business to lessen the effects of climate change. But, despite everything we do to reduce emissions, we will still face changes to the climate. This chapter shows how your company can adapt to the challenges posed.

ADAPTING TO CLIMATE CHANGE – WHAT DOES IT MEAN?

Experts agree that climate change is occurring and we are already feeling some of the impacts. The increased focus on climate change, as seen in Chapter 2, will help to reduce these impacts. But even if emissions could be reduced to nothing, some of the impacts mentioned in Chapter 1 would still occur. Indeed, the Intergovernmental Panel on Climate Change, a collection of scientists tasked to produce objective research on the topic, reveals that, even if the level of greenhouse gas emissions in the atmosphere had stabilised in 2000, the world would still see an increase in average temperature of 0.6 ° C as a result of emissions that have already happened.

Although the impacts will vary between regions and business sectors, your business is bound to be affected in some way. Adjusting your products, services, practices and premises to make your business less vulnerable to the changing climate – and to benefit from business opportunities that open up – is crucial. This is called adapting to climate change.

You might be tempted to focus all your efforts on reducing your carbon dioxide emissions, as this seems the more pressing (and better defined) issue, but emissions reduction and climate change adaptation work should go side by side. So you will have to find the balance between spending time and resources on reducing your company's emissions and putting adaptation measures in place.

Adaptation falls under the category of risk management and management of operations. You might be uncertain about the actual risks to your business and the business case for adapting to climate change, but uncertainty is a big part of thinking about the future. Planning for climate change impacts is no different to any other kind of business planning.

Better information about the potential risks will help you to understand the business case for adaptation. For example, extreme weather events such as flooding and heatwaves are already happening now and are likely to become more frequent in the future. These could affect almost every aspect of your business, including the demand for your products, your ability to source raw materials, the size of your fuel bills and employee retention. It's important to know the risks and opportunities for your company so you can respond to them appropriately.

WHY ADAPT YOUR BUSINESS TO CLIMATE CHANGE?

Axa Insurance found in 2006 that, while 85 per cent of small businesses identify climate change as a problem for the world, only 26 per cent think it is a real threat to them. More recently, the London Assembly found that small businesses are poorly equipped to deal with emergencies like flooding; only a third have a business continuity plan in place, a strategy that anticipates crises that may affect your company and ensures that the business can continue to function if such an event occurs. The report estimates that up to 80 per cent of small businesses without such a plan would be forced to shut down within 18 months of a major event.

In truth, there are numerous risks that your company may have to contend with, not just flooding. At the Federation of Small Businesses Conference 2008, Tom Delay, Chief Executive of the Carbon Trust, identified three categories of risk associated with climate change:

- physical risks to business operations
- compliance risks
- risks to the company's reputation

Physical risks are mainly weather-related and we are already seeing a trend towards warmer summers, wetter winters and more extreme weather events such as storms. Compliance risks relate to the rise in legislation as part of the government's response to climate change. Climate change can also interrupt your service and disgruntled customers may choose to place their orders elsewhere. So it is vital that you consider how you can ensure a consistently high level of customer service, and maintain your business's reputation, in the face of climate change.

Your company's prospects for success in the long term will depend on minimising the effects of these risks and turning them into opportunities.

DEVELOPING AN ADAPTATION STRATEGY

In 2005, UK small businesses were asked how much they knew about climate change. Although some were knowledgeable, 69 per cent knew little or nothing about the consequences for their businesses. By assessing the impacts that climate change may have on your business, you can develop an adaptation strategy that will put your business ahead of the competition and protect it from major risks in the future.

Assess your current situation

To design an effective adaptation strategy, you must first weigh up your current situation. This includes looking at the overall sector in which you work, assessing which organisations you rely on, and which ones rely on you. Consider how your business would be affected by weather events. For example, a survey by insurance company Zurich found that more than 300,000 UK small and medium-sized businesses had been affected by a flood in the past five years, costing the businesses over £800 million. So, think about whether the extreme weather events of the last few years had an impact on your business. Did the floods in the summer of 2007 or the hot weather in 2003 and 2006 affect you?

Help
■ AXA has produced an excellent introduction to the topic entitled 'Preparing for climate change: a practical guide for small businesses'. It can be found in the resources section of the website: www.axa4business.co.uk.

Decide on the scope of your adaptation strategy

Before you start developing an adaptation strategy, there are many factors to consider. For example, how long a time period should it cover? It is prudent for small businesses to plan at least three to five years ahead, but you may also wish to consider other longer-term issues. Whether an issue is a short-term or a long-term consideration will vary according to the sector you are working in and the area in which your company is based. For example, a hotel by the river in York will be more concerned about flooding in the next five years than a similar business in the Scottish highlands.

Also, decide which aspects of the company you are going to consider within your strategy. Will all departments/staff members be involved? Can you work with your suppliers to strengthen your adaptation strategy?

The climate change balancing act

Reducing emissions and adapting to climate change are two sides of the same coin, so it's essential that you consider both. Maintaining a balance between the two can be tricky. Sometimes you will find that actions you take will help with both aspects. For example, installing renewable technologies, such as solar panels, on your building would reduce emissions and also make you less dependent on energy from the National Grid. Your company would therefore be more resilient in the face of an electricity supply failure resulting from adverse weather conditions.

At other times, you may have to make a choice between short-term action to reduce emissions and longer-term action to adapt to climate change. The decision will depend on the associated risks for your business and whether any of the choices will bring a competitive advantage. For instance, you might have to decide between investing in more efficient equipment or better defences against flooding. The equipment may reduce your carbon emissions and make your business more productive, but this may be a small concern if you are expecting severe weather conditions the next winter.

Analyse risks

Once you have decided on the scope of your adaptation strategy, you are ready to start developing it. First, assess the risks that climate change might pose to your business. This requires an understanding of the likely changes in weather in your area. The UK Climate Impacts Programme (UKCIP) has produced maps of predicted temperatures and rainfall levels, as well as other useful resources relating to different regions of the UK. They are available on the UKCIP website (www.ukcip.org.uk) under the heading 'tools to help you' and the subheading 'climate change scenarios for the UK'. Look at 'UKCIP02' on the page that pops up for the weather maps and other helpful resources. These maps were produced with data compiled in 2002. A new set of maps is due to be released in late 2008.

The Business Areas Climate Impacts Assessment Toolkit (BACLIAT) developed by UKCIP can also help you think through the effects of climate change on your business. The simple checklist looks at seven major headings:

1 **logistics** – including supply chain issues, utilities and transport infrastructure;
2 **finance** – including implications for investment, insurance and stakeholder reputation;
3 **markets** – how demand for goods and services may change;
4 **process** – how climate change impacts may affect production processes and service delivery;
5 **people** – including workforce and customers;
6 **premises** – including design of new buildings and maintenance and management of existing ones;
7 **management implications** – how climate change risk analysis can be incorporated into management policies.

The BACLIAT can be found under the 'tools to help you' section of the website (www.ukcip.org.uk), in the subheading 'business assessment tool'.

Assess resilience and identify options

For every risk that you identify, you need to assess the likelihood of it occurring and the vulnerability of your business if it did occur. It is then important to determine your options. These might include reducing the threat to your business or identifying opportunities arising from the risk. For example, a travel agency might find that holidaymakers are booking at the last minute to compensate for uncertain weather conditions. In response, the agency could reduce the discounts that it offered on last-minute bookings and establish more flexible arrangements with the hotels it uses. Alternatively – or even additionally – the agency could focus on increasing bookings in the UK as the weather heats up.

Adaptation in practice: Meridian

Adaptation to climate change is an emerging field and while many businesses are considering its consequences, there are few examples of ideas in practice. However, there are a lot of resources and ideas on how businesses can tackle the problem. So, to encapsulate some of these practical ideas, in addition to case studies, throughout the rest of the chapter, you will see boxes like this that refer to a fictional, small retail clothing firm in London called Meridian. Meridian is looking to develop a climate change adaptation plan, so we will consider some of the risks that Meridian faces and how it can adapt to them.

Let's look at some of the major risks that you, as a business, should consider and what resources are available to help you assess your options. These are grouped under the seven headings of the BACLIAT.

1. Logistics

Water supply

Climate change will have a significant effect on how much water is available, through changes in rainfall levels and also in the way that we use water; hotter weather may result in a greater use of water, for instance, because people wish to water their gardens more. This would result in water shortages and higher water bills, so you need to consider how your company could reduce its reliance on water supplies.

Reducing your company's water usage needn't be difficult or costly. Your company could make savings of up to 30 per cent on water bills by putting no- and low-cost measures in place and an impressive 50 per cent saving by investing in further measures. More information on how you can go about this is available in Chapter 2.

> ### Example: Reducing reliance on mains water supply
> A potted tree business in the East of England was entirely reliant on mains water supply to water its plants. The managing director was concerned about the risk of mains water supply being restricted or cut off completely during a drought, and the effect that this might have on his business. He therefore built a reservoir on-site.

Energy supply

Adverse weather conditions could affect the nation's energy infrastructure. For example, high winds might blow down overhead power lines, cutting off your electricity. By producing your own energy on-site, your business might be able to cope with disruption to the electricity supply.

> ### Example: Installing your own renewable electricity generation
> Andrew Pearce in Rookhope in the Wear Valley received part-funding from the government to install a 6 kilowatt wind

turbine which provides energy for his small business and his household. As well as giving him protection from disruption to the mains electricity supply, he has saved money by reducing fuel bills and exporting excess energy back to the National Grid.

Adaptation in practice: Meridian

Increased energy costs

Risk: Changing weather conditions might make working conditions increasingly uncomfortable for staff unless an air conditioning system was installed. But using air conditioning would also lead to greater carbon emissions, possibly undoing Meridian's attempts to reduce them.

Adaptation: Meridian should consider introducing renewable technologies in its building. While the initial cost might be high, the long-term savings on energy bills could pay back the original investment, particularly with rising energy prices. Air source heat pumps might be the best solution as they can provide cooling as well as heating. If the company were to build new premises, it should try to ensure that energy-efficient design techniques are incorporated to keep heat in during the winter and provide comfortable conditions in summer without the need for a cooling system.

Supply chain issues

Climate change could threaten your supply chain – for example, flooding might affect the factory where your product's components are made or the roads along which they are transported. In the first instance, find out if your suppliers are considering the effects of climate change and putting plans in place to manage those risks. If not, you could avoid disruptions in supply by using more than one supplier or by using a supplier with more than one manufacturing site. You could also consider local sourcing to reduce your vulnerability to transport problems. This would also help to reduce carbon dioxide emissions from transport.

Remember to assess the impacts of climate change not only in the UK but also on any aspects of your supply chain that are based abroad. Rising sea levels and increased storminess could cause damage or disruption to airports or harbours and affect goods that are shipped or flown over.

Help

- 'The changing climate: its impact on the Department for Transport' summarises the potential impacts of climate change on road transport, public transport, aviation and shipping. This document can be found on the Department for Transport website: www.dft.gov.uk (click 'policy, guidance and research', 'science and research' then 'key documents').

Adaptation in practice: Meridian

Impact on supply chain

Risk: Adverse weather conditions might affect Meridian's suppliers. For example, the manufacturing industry in Asia could be affected by issues such as the availability of water, energy supply, and transportation systems. Transport of goods might be affected by longer rainy seasons and rising sea levels. Increased concern about climate change could lead to further legislation with regard to transportation of goods, leading to greater costs.

Adaptation: Meridian should ensure that supply chain issues are fully considered as part of its emergency planning. This might include working with its supplier to have a plan in place to overcome these difficulties or using more than one supplier.

2. Finance

Insurance

AXA research shows that 90 per cent of small businesses are under-insured. Under-insured companies could face significant financial losses if hit by weather events. So consider taking out comprehensive insurance for your premises, contents insurance (for any machinery and stock on-site) and business interruption insurance, which would cover you for any periods when you could not conduct business as normal.

Example: Keeping your insurer happy

The South West Climate Change Impacts Partnership highlights the case of Casella Cel Ltd, which moved its server room to the second floor of their offices because of flood risk. Its insurance company would not provide cover unless this condition was met.

Investment and stakeholder reputation

Investors will find it increasingly important to incorporate climate change risks and opportunities into their analysis and decisions. Therefore, if your company has adapted to climate change, you might encourage investment funding as your reputation with investors and stakeholders improves.

Help

- 'Managing the unavoidable: understanding the investment implications of adapting to climate change' highlights the investment opportunities and risks offered by physical climate change. It can be found in the publications section of the ClimateWise website: www.climatewise.org.uk.

3. Markets

Changing demand in current markets

The changing climate will result in a changing demand for goods and services in most sectors. This is something to bear in mind along with the other factors that affect your customers' demands and behaviour. For example, a report from the South East Climate Change Partnership, a partnership between the public, private and voluntary sectors, notes that hotter summers and milder winters are likely to result in a greater number of both domestic and overseas visitors to the south of England.

So, if you own a tourism business, there may be opportunities for expansion. In particular, the demand for outdoor seating and open spaces would increase.

It will also become increasingly important for you to prove your green credentials; a survey in 2007 showed that 45 per cent of adults consider the impact of their holiday on the environment when choosing their destination and 20 per cent would choose accommodation promoted as green.

Example: Being green, being the best

Compton Pool Farm received a gold award under the Green Tourism Business Scheme for its self-catering cottages. Owner John Stocks says: 'Our vision is to simply offer the best in self-catering family holidays while fully embracing the benefits of a green approach.'

The company insulated and double-glazed its properties and replaced its inefficient heating systems. It has also planted over 200 trees, shrubs and plants and installed a water pump from the lake for animal use and garden irrigation. Customers can also make a voluntary contribution to a local wildlife charity.

The Green Tourism award is advertised on the website and it includes a dedicated webpage on the company's work to green the business. Now they have a high-occupancy rate and turnover has doubled for the business.

Some climate change risks are harder to predict and negotiate. For example, the retail market is extremely climate sensitive. Extreme temperatures at the end of the summer in 1995 led to a decline in the market, with the clothing and footwear industry sustaining a 1.7 per cent reduction in turnover – equivalent to £383 million. On the other hand, certain products sell better during climatic extremes; in the same summer of 1995, beer and wine sales increased significantly. Research by Datamonitor reveals the retail industry is missing out on sales in excess of £4.5 billion per year by not incorporating weather into their decision-making processes.

Adaptation in practice: Meridian

Drop in sales

Risk: Meridian's manager is aware of the risks that climate change presents to the retail market, particularly to clothing stores. Changes in the weather could mean Meridian's products are unsuitable and so the company would miss out on passing trade.

Adaptation: Such variations in sales are difficult to avoid. However, Meridian could attempt to minimise losses by developing innovative selling techniques, including Internet shopping, and by diversifying the products it sells. It should consider the coming changes to the weather both on a yearly basis to decide what stock to buy and, on a daily basis, to decide what to promote.

Help

■ Farming is especially susceptible to changes in climate. A fact sheet produced by Farming Futures suggests a number of adaptations that farmers and growers can make in the face of climate change, including collecting rainwater for use in dry periods and improving soil structure to increase water uptake. This fact sheet, along with case studies, can be found on its website: www.farmingfutures.co.uk.

Example: Farmers bringing the Mediterranean closer to home

The owners of Otter Farm in East Devon realised that increasing temperatures due to climate change offered the opportunity to grow crops traditionally grown in the Mediterranean such as almonds, pecans, apricots and olives. In turn, this helps to reduce emissions by cutting food miles.

The longer, hotter summers are linked to greater unpredictability in weather cycles, so the farm has taken steps to reduce the risk of crop failure by aiming for a greater number of smaller harvests.

Products that reduce emissions

An increasing focus on climate change means there is a growing market for products and services that reduce emissions, such as renewable technologies, energy-efficient products and carbon-offsetting schemes. Could your company take advantage of this expanding market?

Help

■ The Shell Springboard awards celebrate businesses which have developed such products or services. The 2008 winner was Kent-based Carbon8 Systems Ltd, which has developed Accelerated Carbonisation, a process which turns industrial waste into building materials. For ideas about how others are adapting their products, visit the website: www.shellspringboard.com.

Example: New crops for new markets

John Gilliland decided to take advantage of the increasing market for biomass fired heating systems by replacing traditional cereal with willow at Brook Hall Estate in Londonderry. Willow is an energy crop that is also an excellent filter for controlling pollution in water. John now has franchises for six different boiler manufacturers, which allows him to supply boilers as well as wood-chip to customers.

4. Process

Meeting legislative requirements

Legislation will impact on your company's production processes. As mentioned in Chapter 1, restrictions on waste are likely to increase along with disposal charges. But it might be necessary to go beyond mere compliance in order to gain a competitive advantage. Insurance companies, for instance, might look for preventative measures before they offer a policy. Similarly, banks might be less willing to provide loans to businesses that haven't taken climate change risks on board. Further information about meeting legislative requirements can be found in Chapters 2 and 3.

Dealing with weather changes

Changes in temperature and rainfall levels will affect your company's processes and levels of service, so you'll need to instigate quality-control processes to prevent this. For example, manufacturing or chemical engineering companies that undertake technical processes should introduce advanced temperature control in their plants. Builders will also have to protect vulnerable or partly-completed buildings from storm damage.

5. People

Travel

Travel arrangements for your staff could be threatened by changes in weather. In the hot summer of 2003, rail services nationally were delayed a total of 165,000 minutes (compared with just 30,000 in the cooler summer of 2004). This was partly due to a high number of buckled rails, which is more common in hot years. The likelihood of such delays means that you should investigate whether your staff could use alternative means of transport or work at home.

Adaptation in practice: Meridian

Public transport

Risk: Changing weather conditions can lead to uncomfortable conditions on public transport. This is especially likely in London, which suffers from an urban heat island effect, where the centre of the city is several degrees higher than the surrounding countryside. Flooding could even render public transport unusable. Employees might be unable or unwilling to travel to work.

Adaptation: For employees with administrative jobs, Meridian could introduce the option to work from home. Obviously this is not possible for the retail staff. The firm should therefore consider introducing incentives for walking and cycling to work, such as interest-free loans on bicycles, and make it as easy as possible for employees to cycle, by providing storage for bicycles and facilities for showering.

Working conditions

Working conditions for both indoor and outdoor staff might become uncomfortable unless you take steps to prevent this. In the heatwave of 2006, the Federation of Small Businesses issued guidance on steps employers should take during heatwaves. These included ensuring that there is a plentiful supply of drinking water; that windows open and there are blinds in place; and moving desks away from windows and machinery that radiates heat.

Example: Safe and comfortable outdoor working

An Australian firm called DFP Recruitment Services has a policy in place to ensure that, where possible, outdoor workers are protected from excessive exposure to the sun. These include ensuring that employees wear protective clothing and sunscreen, rescheduling heavy work so that it doesn't fall between the hours of 10.00 and 14.00 and giving staff access to cold water and shade.

Health

A changing climate brings health risks. The Department of Health has produced a document outlining the likely effects of climate change on health in the UK. These include an increase in the number of people contracting food-borne diseases due to warmer summers, a greater incidence of tick-borne diseases, and more cases of malaria as popular holiday destinations such as Florida and Southwest Turkey become more susceptible to the disease. However, in the winter months, general health is likely to be better than usual as a result of milder weather during this season.

Make sure your company is prepared for such health risks, by offering adequate health insurance and educating your employees so that they are aware of how to minimise the risk of illness.

6. Premises

Making buildings less vulnerable to climate change impacts

Taking steps to secure your building against weather-related damage is important. In 'Designing for Climate Change', Dr Susan Roaf argues that our 'buildings should be made structurally more sound against an increasingly hostile climate.' As we have seen throughout this chapter, the biggest risks involve flooding in winter and overheating during hot summers. She recommends incorporating the following features into your building:

- wide gutters that are designed to cope with very intense rainfall;
- storm-proofed, well-fixed, roofs;
- shading to exclude all summer sun from within the building;
- strong foundations to cope with clay shrinkage and expansion;
- good natural ventilation through openable windows for summer cooling;
- high levels of thermal mass to keep a building warm or cold without the need for delivered energy use;
- clear, draining cavities in areas of wind-driven rain; and
- wind breaks and structural battening in very exposed areas.

If looking for new premises, some firms might be able to relocate away from the centres of larger cities to avoid the urban heat island effect.

Examples: Smart building to avoid flood damage

City Electrical Factors in Bangor suffers overflows into its car park every time the Afon Adda floods. As well as suffering damage to the car park, the company loses trading days whenever this happens. It has already used insurance money to improve the culvert and the company now intends to rebuild its premises to prevent further problems.

As the largest coastal landowner in Britain, the National Trust has a number of properties at risk from flooding. It has retrofitted one of its activity centres in Norfolk to minimise flood damage, by raising electricity sockets, re-routing cables through the ceiling and covering the floors with washable materials.

Help

■ The Environment Agency website (www.environment-agency.gov.uk) offers a flood map that shows the likelihood of flooding in your area. Just plug your postcode into the search tool on the right-hand side. This website also contains predictions about the availability of water in your region.

Adaptation in practice: Meridian

Damage to property

Risk: Climate change might lead to an increased risk of flooding, which could result in damage to Meridian's property and buildings. According to a recent report about the impacts of climate change on London, a significant proportion of London lies within the floodplain of the River Thames, which means it is exposed to far greater potential damage from flooding than any other urban area in the UK.

Adaptation: Meridian should ensure that it is fully covered for the risk of flooding by its insurance policy. If moving into new premises, it should investigate the risk of flooding in that area and also try to protect stock from damage as far as possible – for example by having stockrooms upstairs rather than in a basement area.

Making buildings comfortable

With increasing temperatures in the summer, it is important to make sure that your offices provide comfortable working conditions for your staff. There are many opportunities to make buildings comfortable that will not have a direct effect on the actual temperature. Such opportunities include changes in clothing and the promotion of air movement through opening windows.

Building new premises

Inevitably there are limitations to what you can do with your existing premises. However, if you are building new premises there are a number of factors that you should take into account as early in the planning stage as possible (it's not easy to change the orientation of your building at a later stage!). Climate change risks should be incorporated into all aspects of a development's design including location, site layout, building structure, ventilation and drainage.

Further information about designing new premises is available in Chapter 7.

Help

- 'Adapting to climate change: a checklist for developments' can be found in the South East Climate Change Partnership (www.climatesoutheast.org.uk) by searching for 'checklist'.

7. Management implications

Staff culture

A positive attitude in staff is crucial to ensure that your business is able to adapt to climate change efficiently, so engage your employees in the adaptation process. Further information about enthusing staff and incentives for green working can be found in Chapter 4.

Legislation

Check that you comply with all relevant legislation (see 'Meeting legislative requirements' on page 135 in this chapter) and, remember, going beyond the minimum compliance can win you new business. Many large organisations require contractors and suppliers to have an environmental management system in place; you can find out more about these systems in Chapter 3.

Incorporating climate change risks into all relevant policies

It is important that adaptation to climate change is included in all business strategy and management. In particular, it should form a major part of your company's business continuity plan. AXA has produced a good guide to business continuity planning for small businesses, which can be accessed in the business continuity section of its website: www.axa4business.co.uk.

Working with other organisations

It's a good idea to work together with other organisations to reduce your company's vulnerability to climate change. Such organisations could include local authorities, which are obliged to provide advice and assistance to businesses about business continuity management under the Civil Contingencies Act 2004. So, consider networking with other similar organisations to share best practice on ideas about adapting to climate change, as well as working towards building resilience in your suppliers to reduce risks further.

Reputation

If you act early to ensure that your business is prepared for a changing climate, you can present your business as a forward-thinking organisation that prepares for the future. This will increase confidence in your company from investors, clients and employees.

Appraise options

Once you've assessed the resilience of your business and what options are available, decide which options to act on. The next step is to prioritise the risks to the business and the relevant adaptation measures. Where are you already experiencing weather-related problems? If you are in a flood-prone area, you would be wise to focus on refurbishing your building with flood-prevention measures before tackling other potential problems.

The costs of adaptation have to be considered in relation to the likely costs if adaptation didn't occur. This may be a difficult issue to visualise, since the costs relate to something that might not happen, but perhaps a large-scale example will help to illustrate the concept. Professor Sir David King, who was the government's Chief Scientific Adviser, notes that the Thames Barrier, which was built at a cost of one billion pounds and has a running cost of about £100 million per annum, has proved to be extremely 'cost effective'; a flood breaking through the barrier would cost about £30 billion and the barrier has been used over six times per year on average over the last six years.

Another UKCIP tool that might be useful is 'Costing the impacts of climate change in the UK'. This provides a method for working out what the costs of climate change impacts might be for an organisation and how to compare these with the costs of adaptation. It can be found on the website (www.ukcip.org.uk) under 'tools to help you' and 'costings tool'.

THINKING LONGER TERM: EVALUATING AND UPDATING YOUR STRATEGY

Adaptation is all about thinking long term; if your adaptation strategy does not prepare for the future, then it serves little purpose. But once you've devised a strategy, you'll have to continue monitoring it to ensure it stays up to date.

In the first instance, assess how successful your decisions have been. Did you miss any opportunities by not acting quickly enough? Has your decision to develop products that respond to the new demands of a changed climate been successful? To evaluate your strategy, you'll need to decide what constitutes success for any action you take and this should be included in the strategy. By having a monitoring process in place, you might pick up earlier on problems and omissions in your strategy and be able to resolve them.

Because information about adaptation is still not as widely available as information on reducing emissions, you should update your adaptation strategy with new projections about climate impacts and new legislation. Your partners and competitors will also supply ideas that should be incorporated into your strategy. You might also wish to extend the scope of your strategy over a longer timescale or involve other aspects of your business.

TAKE THE FIRST STEP

As a first step, consider whether climate change is already affecting your business. If it is, deal with those impacts first. If not, decide what is the most likely impact on your business within the next three to five years.

Then start to consider the potential risks and opportunities that might arise from these changes. The tools mentioned in this chapter may help.

Don't be intimidated by the prospect of developing an adaptation strategy. Not all adaptation measures are costly or difficult. They can be as simple as relaxing your dress code and opening windows during hot weather. Look at what policies and procedures you can implement in the short term to improve the resilience of your business. And remember that climate change is a long-term problem, so you still have time to adapt your strategy as new challenges arise.

ACTION CHECKLIST

Developing your plan	Done
Assess your current situation	
Decide on the scope of your adaptation strategy	
Analyse the risks to your business	
Assess the resilience of your business and what options you have to tackle risks	
Appraise and prioritise those risks and options	
Implement your adaptation strategy	
Things to do in the longer term	Done
Monitor your adaptation strategy	
Evaluate if your actions have been successful	
Update your strategy with new information and ideas	

RECOMMENDED LINKS

The UKCIP website (www.ukcip.org.uk) should be your first port of call. It includes maps of predicted temperatures and precipitation levels in different regions of the UK and links to a number of regional documents. It also contains the Business Areas Climate Impacts Assessment Tool (BACLIAT), which will help you analyse the risks and options for your business.

AXA (www.axa4business.co.uk) has produced several excellent guides for adapting to climate change in small businesses and developing business continuity plans.

Chapter 7

Making your premises sustainable

Chapter 1 introduced many of the reasons why we need to tackle existing environmental problems. Too often we procrastinate and put off a response to these problems for another day. But sometimes we have a good excuse to take action and moving to a new building or refurbishing an existing one provides an opportunity to make environmental improvements.

By making sure your building is sustainable you can greatly improve your green credentials from the outset and gain a head start in becoming a truly green business. Even if you're not moving offices, you may want to look at your plans for refurbishing your premises. The information in this chapter will help you to integrate sustainable aspects into any major changes you undertake.

In many ways, the location, design and physical characteristics of your building set the upper limit of your environmental performance and having sustainable premises makes it much easier to manage, control and reduce your environmental impact. Here are some examples of how you could achieve this.

- Monitoring how many lights are left on unnecessarily can become a thing of the past if you install a combination of motion or light sensors with timer switches/programmers.
- You won't have to use lights at all for much of the year if you choose a building that maximises the use of natural light and where workstations are situated close to the windows.
- A push to encourage the use of public transport is far more likely to succeed if your building is well served by buses and trains.
- Heating is a major cause of carbon dioxide emissions from buildings. Refurbishing your building to improve its thermal properties and air-tightness can massively reduce your heating requirements, making the management of energy use a much less daunting prospect.

As well as having a smaller environmental impact and lower running costs in the winter, a well-designed, energy-efficient building will be better protected from climate change impacts in summer such as more frequent episodes of overheating. As summers get hotter, working conditions in poorly designed offices will become increasingly uncomfortable. Well-designed, climate-proof premises will become easier to sell or let. Long-term running costs, including fuel bills and insurance, will be lower and the future asset value higher.

The building's occupants, too, will benefit from an improved physical environment, so it's always useful to investigate changes even if you rent a property. Research has shown that people work better in buildings with plenty of natural lighting and ventilation and where they have some control over the environment. They are more relaxed, more productive and less subject to minor illness and absenteeism.

Absenteeism due to respiratory illnesses can be reduced by up to 35 per cent by increasing outdoor ventilation, and further research has shown that doubling the rate of natural ventilation increases worker efficiency by two per cent. It is also believed that exposure to natural daylight increases productivity, although there are no exact figures to quantify this.

There are powerful arguments for energy conservation in your business because a 25 per cent reduction in energy consumption can bring impressive savings but a much bigger impact can be made by increasing productivity. An increase of just one per cent in productivity could yield fifty times as much in extra profit.

Your business premises are the flagship of your organisation. Improving the environmental performance of your premises gives a bold statement that you are an organisation with principles that delivers on its commitments.

HOW TO USE THIS CHAPTER

In this chapter we will help you to understand how your building impacts upon the environment and show you ways of reducing that impact. The options open to you will depend on whether you are:

- choosing new premises;
- moving in and want to make basic changes;
- taking an opportunity to make more substantial improvements to a new or current building;
- building something new from scratch.

We recommend you start by reading the section on 'Choosing new premises' (see page 147). Although this is aimed largely at organisations which are looking for a new business site, many of the suggestions included are founding principles to bear in mind whatever your current circumstances. Then the section you choose to read next will depend on your specific situation. Here's a rough breakdown of what each contains.

- **Moving in or tackling the basics** is aimed at businesses which are either about to occupy new premises and want to ensure they have covered the basics or those which want to make basic changes to their existing premises. It outlines simple, cost-effective measures that you ought to consider if you haven't already taken them on board.
- **Making further improvements** provides useful information for businesses which are ready to make more substantial changes; this includes businesses which are moving into a new building that requires substantial refurbishment and those which have plans to refurbish their existing building. You'll find it helpful to return to this section whenever you are planning work on your building, as it's always a good time to make environmental improvements.

■ **Specifying a new building** covers the important topics for businesses which are designing and building a new site.

CHOOSING NEW PREMISES

When choosing new business premises you will almost certainly have a budget in mind that you need to stick to and a fair idea of the size and type of place you're looking for. Nevertheless, you may still face a range of options.

The key point is that two otherwise similar properties can differ greatly in their carbon dioxide emissions and their potential to be green. There are a number of basic things to consider.

Getting the temperature right

The basic design and construction of the building will often have the biggest influence on the amount of energy you use. Space heating generally accounts for more than 50 per cent of a building's carbon impact and the thermal efficiency of the walls, roof, floor, windows and doors can mean the difference between spending thousands of pounds a year or spending nothing on space heating.

Most heat will be lost directly through the building fabric itself. Bolt-on renewable energy technologies make the headlines these days. But it is the humble old roof, walls, floors, doors and windows that have the biggest impact on energy use.

When choosing a new building, consider these basic characteristics. If the walls and roof currently have no insulation, investigate whether insulation can be installed. In larger premises, it may be worth hiring a private firm to identify the best way to insulate the building.

Walls

Walls generally account for the largest area of heat loss in buildings – typically nearly 10 per cent of the heat lost from a building. However, if your premises have walls that transmit heat quickly (such as solid stone walls or walls with an uninsulated cavity), this figure can be proportionately higher. Buildings with walls that transmit heat quickly are harder to keep warm in winter and keep cool in the heat of summer. Uninsulated older buildings will fall into this category, so you might prefer to choose a more modern property. If so, find out about the cavity in the walls. Wall cavities are more commonplace in buildings built after 1945, where the space between the inner and outer walls was designed to keep out damp. Filling it with insulation (often referred to as cavity wall insulation) will significantly help to keep heat in.

Roofs

In a typical construction, around 20 per cent of a building's heat is lost through the roof. Therefore, fitting loft insulation of 300mm or more in a building is one of the easiest and most cost-effective ways of reducing heat loss. Find out if the building has a loft and, if so, what level of insulation it contains.

Floors

Although we think of heat rising, floors can also be a problem, particularly if there are gaps or cracks. Nearly 10 per cent of heat is lost through the ground floor of a building, so find out if this has insulation as well.

Draught-stripping

While it is important to keep your building well-ventilated, uncontrolled ventilation through poorly fitted doors and windows not only costs money but can make working conditions very uncomfortable in windy conditions

Heating, ventilation and air conditioning

The type of fuel that a building uses to provide heating, ventilation and air conditioning is crucial to its overall carbon dioxide emissions. Electricity is by far the most carbon-intensive and expensive form of heating. By comparison, gas produces less than half the amount of carbon dioxide per kilowatt hour (kWh). Therefore, look for buildings that are heated by gas or where you may be able to replace an old electric heating system.

Windows

Another factor to consider is the heat gains and losses through windows. Single-glazed panes of glass are often a major source of heat loss in winter. Newer, double- and triple-glazed windows minimise heat loss and most of the current energy-efficient windows are coated with a metallic film that decreases the amount of heat coming through in summer, too.

Fuel type and carbon dioxide emissions

Unless you use a renewable technology to heat your premises, you will emit carbon dioxide every time you turn your heating on. The amount you emit, though, depends on the type of fuel you use for the system. The following table shows you how much carbon dioxide each of the major heating fuels emits.

Fuel Type	kg CO_2/ kWh
Grid electricity*	0.527
Natural gas	0.206
Gas oil	0.265
Diesel	0.263
Coal	0.346
Liquid petroleum gas	0.225

* The mix of energy supplying the grid will result in this figure varying from year to year.

For every 1,000 kilowatt hours (kWh) you use in electricity, you will emit 5,270 kilograms of carbon dioxide (kg CO_2). If you are using natural gas, for the same amount of kilowatt hours, you might only emit 2,060 kg CO_2, depending on the efficiency of your boiler.

Furthermore, heating, ventilation and air conditioning systems, often called HVAC systems, in existing buildings can be woefully inefficient, so look out for newer, more efficient systems that have become mainstream in recent years. Premises built or renovated after 6 April 2006 fell under the current Building Regulations which required significantly more efficient HVAC systems. Further information on replacing your heating system can be found in the 'Making further improvements' section below.

Energy Performance Certificates

In compliance with European legislation, the government has introduced Energy Performance Certificates (EPCs) for both homes and commercial properties. Any time you buy or rent a new property, the agent is required to give you a copy of the EPC. This certificate uses a rating system like the one you find on fridge-freezers, with a colour-coded A–G rating. The closer the rating is to 'A', the better the property will perform. The detail of the EPC will tell you how much carbon dioxide on average the building will emit throughout the year and what you should expect to pay on your energy bills.

The certificate also includes a report on energy-efficiency measures that could improve the performance of the building. It will start with the most cost-effective options and indicate both how much it would cost to install the relevant measure and what sort of savings you should expect to make. It also indicates what new rating the building would achieve once each measure is put in place.

While it's useful for you, as the occupier of the building, to understand how the building was constructed and what energy-efficiency measures are in place, the EPC will give a more thorough understanding of how it will perform. The document will also be extremely useful when you are negotiating prices for any improvements.

Help

■ The Government Department of Communities and Local Government is responsible for implementing EPCs. For more information, visit its dedicated website: www.communities.gov.uk/epbd.

Locating for minimal staff travel

Transport to and from your place of work will generally be a major source of your company's environmental impact. The location of your building and the distance that your staff, visitors and customers have to travel should therefore be a top consideration.

Key questions are:

■ how are people going to get to the building?
■ where are the nearest bus or train stops?
■ how frequent are the services?

- is the building on a cycle-friendly route?
- does it have facilities for cyclists, e.g. secure bike storage and showers or changing rooms?

In urban areas, public transport is often the quickest and most convenient way to travel. Nevertheless, the car still dominates the daily commute to work. You can help your staff to reduce the environmental impact of their commute by locating close to public transport links that run frequently and on time. Also, by making working hours more flexible, you can accommodate bus and train times.

Some basic research of the local public transport facilities should be sufficient, although if you need further information you could contact your council's transport planning service.

Public transport should be encouraged where possible. However, perhaps the ultimate mode of sustainable transport is the bicycle. The National Cycle Network offers over 12,000 miles of walking and cycle routes on traffic-free paths, quiet lanes and traffic-calmed roads. Also, check if there are facilities for cyclists on the premises; if there aren't, see if there are suitable places where they could be installed. Facilities could include the provision of basic cycle racks, changing facilities or even showers and a dedicated drying space for wet clothes. Cycle racks can be installed in a variety of forms outside buildings and take up relatively little space.

Help

- National Cycle Network maps are available free on the Sustrans website (www.sustrans.org.uk), so take a look and see whether your potential business premises are near to a route. Some cities might also have a cycling map, which indicates routes that are more cycle-friendly, even if they are not designated cycle paths, as well as roads and junctions to avoid.

Maximising use of natural daylight

Lighting is a major source of energy use for businesses, accounting for 20 to 40 per cent of electricity use. Also, excess heat from inefficient lighting systems can often make staff hot and uncomfortable. We've given information on lighting systems on pages 157 and 161, and show how you can manage your artificial lighting efficiently.

When choosing a new building, however, one of the most important things to look for is how the building makes use of natural light. Effective use of natural light minimises your energy requirement and, as many people prefer to work in natural light, it can improve staff morale and increase productivity.

Making the most of natural daylight is not simply a case of looking for big windows. Locating desks and working spaces close to windows is usually beneficial. Make sure, though, that the workspace does not become too draughty or, if south-facing, receive too much unhelpful glare and heat on a sunny day.

The height of the window in a room is also important, as this effects how much light penetrates the building. Unobstructed windows will allow more light into spaces and therefore skylights might be a good option (make sure they're fitted with blinds to avoid problems with glare).

Considering the layout

Think about how the air will flow through the building. Will there be draughty or stuffy areas? These can create unpleasant working environments either because the temperature or humidity is difficult to control or there is a build-up of pollutants. Ensuring that there is adequate ventilation where staff will work, either naturally through windows or through an installed ventilation system, will help to avoid these problems.

It's also important that space is set aside at your premises to allow waste to be sorted and stored on-site prior to collection and disposal. How your waste collection and disposal facilities are set up will likely affect the way that your employees dispose of waste – if recycling can be made easy it will quickly become the norm at your workplace. For more information on how to dispose of waste, see Chapter 2.

Preparing for future upgrades

Long-term improvements to the premises may not be top of your list of priorities when choosing offices. After finding new, sustainable offices at an affordable rent and getting over the hassles of moving, you will be looking forward to getting back to business as usual. However, it's a good idea to consider the future potential of the building. Will it still meet your requirements in five year's time, for instance?

When considering improvements, such as decorating, wiring or lighting, are there any greener alternatives or additional sustainability features that could be introduced. These could include:

- new or improved windows;
- scope for improving natural ventilation and cooling;
- improving natural daylight through other means, like daylighting tubes;
- making conditions more comfortable by insulating outside walls and adding new partition walls, which will help to keep temperatures even by absorbing heat during the day and giving it off overnight.

The following list is helpful when comparing potential new offices.

State of windows

- **Double glazing** – if the window frames are in a good state of repair but single-glazed, could they easily be upgraded to accommodate sealed doubled-glazed panels? The main consideration is whether the frames will be able to accommodate 'thicker' double glazed windows, which are often 24mm thick.
- **Secondary glazing** – would the depth of the window opening allow you to fit secondary glazing? Secondary glazing introduces another window on the inside of the existing windows and is often cheaper than replacing the glazing. Another benefit is that it can be done as and when there is an opportunity to do so and on a window-by-window basis. Secondary glazing also offers insulation from noise as well (ideally, you would need a 200mm gap for this).
- If the windows are in a bad state of repair, could these be replaced with energy-efficient, double-glazed units as part of the negotiation with the landlord for the new tenancy?

Improving ventilation

A general explanation of passive ventilation, along with other passive design features, can be found under 'Specifying a new building' on page 174.

- Passive ventilation generally relies on the principle of hot air rising, so good ventilation will require a path that cooler, outside air at lower levels can flow up as it is heated. Is there potential to put in extract grilles in the ceiling, which would require ducting above to a ridge or roof vent? Could inlet grilles also be put into walls or doors at a lower level?
- If you have access to opposite sides of the building, are there windows on both sides which could provide some 'cross-flow' ventilation in windy conditions?
- If the office space is on the upper floor, is there potential to consider a wind-assisted stack ventilation? This would require planning permission, but one such 'chimney' unit would allow fresh air to enter and stale air to exit the room it serves.

Improving natural light

It is important to review both the amount and quality of natural daylight available to staff. Often southern light can be too bright and create glare, while northern light is softer and more diffuse. Therefore, check if there's scope for introducing any of the following:

- new window openings in wall and roofs, particularly on the northern side of the building;
- daylighting tubes which introduce daylight through an opaque cover on the roof and bring it down through reflective 'pipes' and into the room through a flush mounted ceiling 'light'. These would require access to the roof and any intervening floors, but integrated daylighting/passive ventilation units are available which would enable two benefits from one installation;
- window louvres and light shelves fitted to the outside of windows to restrict glare and excessive heat from the sun on southern windows.

Improving comfort

Improving comfort for staff could involve installing more efficient and responsive heating and cooling measures as well as better ventilation and lighting.

- Can time and temperature controls be readily added to the heating system?

■ If the building is likely to overheat, could additional thermal mass be added if new internal partitions or walls are being considered? If so, using cladding made from particular natural materials such as wood-fibre or reedboard could have the effect of regulating internal humidity as well.

MOVING IN OR TACKLING THE BASICS

Whether you have chosen new premises for your business or are doing a basic refit of your existing buildings, there are a number of basic improvements you can make when you move in that are important to the building's overall sustainability.

This section covers the basic equipment, fixtures and fittings you'll need to install in any new premises. However, moving into a new building is an excellent opportunity to make more substantial improvements and refurbishments. Therefore, do look at the next section on 'Making further improvements' (see page 160) to see if any of the refurbishments listed there could be applied at the moving-in stage.

Moving is a chance for a new start and many businesses see it as an opportunity to kit out the new site. If you are a growing business or the space is completely different from your previous premises, there can be good reasons to invest in new equipment, furniture and decor. But sustainable businesses will make use of what they have already. So before you're tempted to grab the Ikea catalogue or ring up Dell, have a quick look at what's sitting in the old office and hold on to all the items that still meet your needs.

Once you've allocated all the furniture and equipment from the old office, you may still need a few new things. Check out the section on 'Purchasing' in Chapter 2 (see pages 27 and 41), which gives you all the principles to consider when making purchases for your business.

Draught stripping

Although insulating your building will minimise the amount of heat lost through your walls and roof, it can be a disruptive and costly change. At the very least, though, when moving in you should seal up any cracks or openings in the building. These are often found around skirting and roof joins as well as around windows and door frames. A simple check to decide whether a window needs draught stripping is to use the back of your hand to feel if there is any air movement on a windy day. If there is, then draught stripping is important. This job may have been done for in the past, but check that it is in good condition and that it hasn't got damp.

Take control

Checking the controls you use for your building services can be done at any time, but when you move into a new building it is very easy to switch to better controls. All buildings have controls for their services and the most common are:

■ heating and cooling
■ lighting
■ ventilation

If you are working in a manufacturing company, you will have many additional controls and this is the perfect time to think about upgrading them.

There are many things to bear in mind with any type of system control. First, buildings rarely need all of the services on all of the time, so installing timer controls is the first step to reducing overuse. Many offices can operate on fairly basic timer controls as long as you can turn the service on before staff arrive and turn it off afer they leave and at weekends. However, some offices and other buildings will benefit from seven-day programmable timers which can turn services on or off at different times of the day to take account of how many people are working there and how long the building takes to warm up and cool down. Ideally, you would want to set a basic programme on your controls and use a boost control when you need a bit extra. For example, on a cold day you could turn on the boost control to provide an extra hour of heating.

For bigger premises, it's a good idea to use zone controls. These allow you to put in different programmes for different areas of the building. Consider zone controls if your business sees variations in:

■ occupancy;
■ temperature requirements;

■ ventilation and use of external doors;
■ number of floors (particularly if the top floor is poorly insulated).

Heating and cooling

In addition to timer, boost and zone controls for heating and cooling, thermostats are your other consideration. Ideally, you would have a thermostat in every room and they should be kept away from draughts or heat sources (such as radiators and equipment).

In addition, you will want to set programmes that reflect the necessary temperature for the work that is going on. The Carbon Trust recommends that you set your thermostat at:

■ 10°C in a warehouse setting;
■ 13°C in an area where people are undertaking physical work;
■ 19–20°C for office activity.

Temperature controls should also be set for any cooling system you have. Make sure that the minimum temperature at which the cooling system turns on is above the maximum temperature for the heating system to switch off. Again, the Carbon Trust suggests that cooling systems start at 24°C. Frequently, businesses do not view these systems together, which results in both being on at the same time.

Further information on more sophisticated controls can be found in 'Making further improvements' under 'Replacing the heating system' (see page 168).

Lighting

Needless use of lighting is a major culprit of wasted energy. A survey concluded that 27 per cent of the lighting used by businesses is wasted. However, this can be eliminated quickly by the use of effective lighting-control systems.

Lighting controls can greatly reduce your energy bills and carbon footprint by providing the right quantity of light as and when required. Efficient and cost-effective lighting-control systems are now well established, reliable and easy to install. Motion sensors are perhaps the most well known lighting controls, but built-in light sensing photocells are also increasingly popular. These photocells measure the amount of natural light available and tell the lights whether or not to switch on and at what levels of brightness, ensuring an optimally lit workplace at all times.

Ventilation

In addition to time and temperature controls, ventilation systems may need to be set to control humidity, dust and carbon dioxide. Significant savings can be made if these controls are linked with variable fan settings which allow you to run the system at different speeds depending on the amount of ventilation that the building needs. Individual ventilation fans can also be set with occupancy sensors (see page 157 under 'Lighting').

Are you poisoning your staff?

We touched on the subject of toxicity in Chapter 2. This requires further exploration when moving into new premises. Computers, photocopiers and many other types of equipment emit chemicals such as volatile organic compounds, but new carpets, furniture and paint can also pump chemicals into the environment that you'd rather not have hanging around. Volatile organic compounds, otherwise known as VOCs, include:

■ formaldehyde – found in chipboard, fabrics, tissues and paints;
■ benzene – found in glues, floor coverings and photocopiers;
■ xylene and toluene – found in Visual Display Units (monitors); and
■ acetone – found in pre-printed paper.

As there's usually no ingredients list on the equipment and furniture we buy, it can be difficult to avoid VOCs. However, it's advisable to look for alternatives when buying products, e.g. choose natural paints over synthetic paints, and solid wood furniture with natural oils rather than wood-waste products (MDF, chipboard, etc.), which use a lot of glue or resin. More products are coming on to the market that specifically keep the amount of VOCs to a minimum. Look out for these types of products and, if you can't find them, ask your supplier what's in their products and what alternatives are available.

The only way to avoid all VOCs, though, would be to leave your business empty, since humans themselves emit over 150 VOCs, our way of getting rid of toxic chemicals. Tempting as that might sound on a Monday morning, it probably isn't workable in the long run. Instead, ensure that the building is properly ventilated and take a look at the section on natural ventilation on page 177 to make sure you're doing all you can to air it out. If you rely on a mechanical ventilation system, make sure it's kept clean and in good repair. That way, you can avoid many of the toxic chemicals we've mentioned as well as any bacteria that might grow in the system.

After that, there are other items you might want to add to your list of new purchases, one of which is houseplants. Many houseplants have air-purifying qualities: the common peace lily, for instance, helps to removes VOCs found in varnishes, adhesives, synthetic furnishings and computer screens. Many of the hardiest houseplants, such as spider plants and rubber plants, will help keep the air clear, so even those without a green thumb can benefit. Two to three plants for every 10 square metres is ideal. Plants should be located in your 'personal breathing zone', so set them on your desk if you're in an office.

Other things to avoid in a healthy work environment are mould and rotting food.

- Mould: Persistently damp conditions can cause mould to develop. The spores from these are well recognised as a human allergen. Creating warm and dry conditions will often alleviate condensation problems unless there is a building-related issue such as blocked gutters causing an outside wall to be damp for long periods of time.
- Rotting food: This, too, can produce fungal spores if waste food is left for too long. So, be particularly careful if you intend to compost food waste.

Help
- The expert in this field is BC Wolverton who worked for NASA on skylabs, an environment that really can't benefit from opening the window. Check out his book on *How To Grow Fresh Air: 50 Houseplants That Purify Your Home Or Office* (Orion, £9.99).

MAKING FURTHER IMPROVEMENTS

In the last section we focused on small improvements that every business should investigate when moving into a new building. But there are many other measures you can take which will lead to greater savings, both environmentally and financially. And it makes sense to take these on board when moving into new premises, or when planning repairs or even a full refurbishment, to help to bring an existing building up to the best standards available. Ideally, read this section in conjunction with Chapter 6 on adapting to climate change. Any major improvements should consider the risks of climate change as well as attempts to prevent it.

The upgrades and refurbishments we suggest in this section vary both in terms of cost and the level of disruption they cause. For example, fitting dedicated low-energy lights needn't cause disruption and is very cost effective, whereas insulating internal walls could involve all or part of the building being empty for a number of days or weeks.

How many improvements you decide to make will depend on several factors, most of them financial. Whether you own or rent the building you work in will have a major influence on the sort of work you will want to undertake.

If you are renting from a landlord, you will ideally want a payback period within the terms of your lease to make the investment worth doing. If the payback period is longer than the length of your lease, you may be able to negotiate with the landlord for a reduced rent or a contribution towards the investment, on the basis that it will be adding value to the building. Check your lease to find out if you have the right to make these changes and whether you need permission from your landlord. Your landlord may also approach you with improvements that he or she would like to make. This is a great opportunity to suggest environmental improvements that might not be cost effective for you to make yourself.

If you are undertaking a comprehensive refurbishment to bring your building up to the best possible standard, it's best to consult an architect or building professional regarding the feasibility and cost of different options. An architect with experience in this area will be able to take a holistic approach to your building's energy efficiency and sustainability and ensure that you do not waste money on expensive but largely ineffectual improvements. Remember, by making changes to a building, you can dramatically change the way it functions and its level of comfort. It is vital to consult professionals to make sure that the building will be improved as planned, not undermined by lack of attention to detail in some areas (such as making a breathable wall non-breathable by applying the wrong paint, lining or cladding material).

Upgrading the lighting systems

Lighting is an essential fact of life for businesses and it is possible to cut lighting bills by 50 per cent or more through a variety of lighting-replacement measures. The potential for saving energy through lighting is enormous and can be achieved with technologies that are readily available and which provide a very quick payback on your initial investment.

According to the Carbon Trust, there are countless instances of companies persisting with inefficient lighting because they simply don't realise how much energy is wasted through common, slightly older forms of lighting. For example, the Carbon Trust advises that it is generally more cost effective to replace lighting that is over ten years old than to keep it in place.

Case study: Irn Bru

The Irn Bru drinks manufacturer A.G. Barr recently managed to reduce company lighting costs by 65 per cent through an overhaul of its lighting systems, providing a return on its initial investment in less than two years.

So how can these savings be achieved? Converting your lighting installations to energy-efficient types of lamps and control gear could save up to 50 per cent or more of the electricity consumed without reducing lighting quality and, in many cases, lighting quality would be improved.

Standard incandescent bulbs can be easily replaced by 'energy saving' light bulbs found in any supermarket or office supply store, and offer one of the cheapest and easiest ways to save energy. The latest generation of 'energy saving' light bulbs, sometimes called compact fluorescent lamps, are a vast improvement on their flickering, slow-reacting and dull predecessors, and provide the same quality of light as standard bulbs.

Fluorescent lighting: Bringing yourself up to date

If you use fluorescent tube lighting, check out the many new and improved lamp types, which include T5 linear fluorescent and high-pressure sodium, each providing opportunities to reduce energy consumption.

Companies using older style fluorescent lamps are most likely to be able to benefit from replacing lighting systems. The inefficient T12 (1.5″ radius) and T8 (1 inch radius) fluorescent bulbs have a useful life of between 6,500 and 8,000 hours. However, they will probably continue to operate for twice that time, usually without anyone realising that the efficiency has decreased dramatically.

The good news is that T5 tubes, which are more efficient, can be installed in older T8 and T12 fittings, despite being shorter. To do this, you will need to purchase an adapter. Furthermore, newer light installations have a much longer life than their predecessors, and so don't need to be replaced as often, resulting in lower maintenance costs.

Whether using compact or tubular fluorescent lighting, it is possible to obtain lamps that use a daylight spectrum to give a similar type of light to natural light. If you are installing a completely new lighting system, choose the most efficient one available that doesn't give more lighting than is necessary and consider how much control you can introduce into the system. Basic information on controls is available in 'Moving in or tackling the basics' on page 156, but the overall consideration is to make your lighting system as controllable and user-friendly as possible. So check out what controls there are for timing and adjusting to light levels and how easy they are to use.

Help

■ The Carbon Trust has a Lighting Implementation Guide on its website (www.carbontrust.co.uk). Click on the 'solutions' tab, followed by the 'save energy' section. Under the 'take action' heading, you will find the guide. This takes you through all the necessary steps of a major lighting refurbishment, or you can select the 'Lamp Selection Tool' which gives information on all the different types of lights available so you can find one to suit your needs. A light with a high 'luminous efficacy' will be very efficient and a high 'colour rendering' will be brighter, similar to daylight.

Replacing glazing

More efficient buildings will have windows that limit the amount of heat passing through them but that still allow light to pass through freely. Window technology has come on in leaps and bounds in recent years: double glazing, triple glazing and heavy gas filled layers on windows allow less heat to escape while still letting in light. Also, new coatings mean that the amount of heat leaving the building through the glass can be minimised while the amount of light remains almost unaffected.

Whether you are choosing, building or refurbishing a property, look out for the British Fenestration Rating Council (BFRC) rating for windows. The BFRC rates windows based on their overall energy performance. The highest A-rated windows will minimise the heat lost while letting in lots of light. In fact, the best windows actually lead to an overall gain of energy, saving you money on heating and lighting.

Help

■ The BFRC website (www.bfrc.org) has an excellent searchable database of windows.

Minimising the negative effects of solar gain and glare

The problem with solar gain is that it's welcome for much of the year, but it can create too much heat in some buildings in the summer. In this situation, shading is important to reduce the need for cooling. Shutters and blinds are a low-cost solution. For some buildings, careful planting of deciduous trees (or climbing plants in conservatory areas) on the south side of the building can also help to resolve this problem. These trees will provide shelter from the sun in the summer months but still allow natural light through to the windows when they lose their leaves in the winter.

Alternatively, 'external light shelves' can be positioned to stop light from the summer sun directly entering through windows while still allowing the winter sun (which comes in at a lower angle) through. These are typically made of louvres or slats.

Some buildings are designed so that the upper floors slightly overhang the lower ones, or roof eaves overhang the top storey, leading to the same result. External light shelves can therefore be a good option for any refurbishment or new-build project, limiting both light glare and excessive solar heat gain.

Internal light shelves mounted to the inside of tall windows have a similar effect but also bounce visible light up towards the ceiling, which reflects it down deeper into the interior of a room.

Blinds can be installed above and below the light shelves so that users are able to adjust the brightness of the room for individual comfort at different times of day.

Metering

Many business premises have only basic electricity, and possibly, gas meters which can be read manually. As they are typically read on behalf of the energy supply company once a year, quarterly bills are often estimated. Unless they are read more frequently, they will give no indication of the pattern of energy consumption.

This is far from ideal if you are looking to reduce the amount of energy you use. As mentioned in Chapter 2, any attempts to reduce energy use are more likely to succeed if you can see the fruits of your efforts. Also, proper energy monitoring equipment, energy display units or smart meters are essential for identifying where energy is being wasted and the most cost-effective way to change this. Put simply: 'you can't manage what you can't measure.'

Smart meters are an emerging technology, producing automatic, regular meter data for small electricity and gas sites. The Carbon Trust has run smart meter trials which showed that small and medium-sized businesses can make significant energy savings through deploying smart meters and using the data for energy management.

Smart metering is not yet widely available, although some new buildings may already have the technology installed. If you are refurbishing, ask your energy supplier whether they can provide this facility. There are also many private companies that offer smart metering services and you can often analyse the data via their websites.

Energy monitoring programme

Energy monitoring makes it possible to set targets, quantify energy use reductions, prioritise actions and ensure that you are saving the maximum amount of energy and money. If your energy use as a business is a large proportion of your overheads, you will want to undertake a full energy monitoring and targeting programme. This involves having half-hourly meter readings to provide good-quality data. Larger electricity sites have half-hourly metering as standard, allowing the occupiers to identify where waste is occurring.

Half-hourly meters are automatically read by the system and produce regular consumption data, sometimes available online. This route is most suitable for bigger companies with several sites which can take advantage of bulk electricity purchase tariffs. However, gas and smaller electricity sites typically have less regular metering and may require upgrading to get higher-quality data.

Minimising water use

We highlighted the importance of water-saving technologies and devices in Chapter 2. Bear these in mind when choosing, building or refurbishing new premises. Business premises that use these technologies in conjunction with a good water management plan can cut their water usage by up to 80 per cent, compared to inefficient similar-sized sites, thereby reducing their environmental impact and increasing profits. As a guide, the Building Research Establishment recommends water usage of below 5 cubic metres ($5m^3$) per person per year as best practice.

If water use is particularly high in your business, check that you are not literally pouring money away. Regular monitoring (as with energy) and fitting a leak-detection system will ensure this doesn't happen.

For all types of business premises, fitting flow restrictors on all forms of tap and shower can lead to large savings in water use. Installing aerator taps can reduce water flow by up to 80 per cent and electronic sensor taps or push taps prevent wastage and flooding that arise when taps are left running.

Standard flush toilets with cisterns of six or more litres can be replaced to make big water savings. Newer, environmentally-friendly models use a fraction of this amount and tend to have variable dual flush levels. If these are not an option, then simple 'hippo' water bags can be placed in the cistern to reduce the amount of water that comes through. These are generally available free of charge from your water company, but it is important to test these on each cistern to ensure the cistern still does its job properly. If you find that, after fitting a 'hippo', two flushes rather than one are required, then you will need to introduce a smaller version.

Urinal controls, such as presence detectors, can significantly reduce water consumption by ensuring they flush only when needed. Indeed, waterless urinals can reduce water use further. These systems are available as both a complete unit or as systems that can be fitted to standard bowls and troughs.

To enhance your environmental credentials even further, you may want to investigate ways to capture, reuse and recycle water. Rainwater harvesting systems are readily available, easy to install and can substitute more than 50 per cent of your current mains water usage. Greywater recycling systems are also available for reusing the waste water. Most systems will reuse all waste water except for sewage and toxic waste.

Help
■ Speak to your water supplier about free or subsidised services they offer for reducing water use.

Internal walls
If you are erecting internal walls as partitions, you may want to consider timber stud walling that uses specialist breathable building boards based

on natural materials in order to make a building more comfortable. These include wood-fibre board or reed boards and have the benefit of adding some thermal mass to an otherwise thermally lightweight wall. This means they will store heat and give it off slowly as the building cools down, helping to regulate temperature. Many natural and breathable walls also regulate humidity.

With these materials, it is important to use natural paints to enable them to breathe. A synthetic paint provides a fairly impenetrable barrier that doesn't allow the wall to breathe and, in some cases, could cause moisture to be trapped behind this barrier.

Wrapping up your building

One highly efficient and undisruptive improvement is cavity wall insulation. It can be installed in any building that has an inner and outer wall with a cavity between them. This is one of the easiest upgrades you can make and, typically, it is one of the most cost-effective steps to reducing carbon dioxide emissions.

If you have solid walls, there are a number of internal and external insulation methods that will improve the performance of your building. Reputable building engineers, architects and construction firms will help you to find the most appropriate methods. Look for contractors which have worked on other sustainable refurbishment projects to ensure they have the necessary experience. For interlay wall insulation, choose a system that comes with a good warranty period (between 10 and 20 years) and which is backed up by the manufacturer.

Loft or roof insulation is another cost-effective investment, providing you have space on the top floor and access to the roof. If you are short on roof space, there are many new insulation technologies that allow you to get the same level of insulation from a much thinner product.

Pipework should also be insulated, so check whether this has been done and what condition it's in. Insulating heating and hot water pipes reduces unnecessary heat loss and is very cost effective; insulating cold pipes minimises condensation and the incidence of freezing in some unheated areas. Pipes outside of the building should be weatherproofed and insulated to 50mm, and internal pipes insulated to 25mm. Make sure that valves and flanges have removable insulation so that you can still maintain them.

Replacing the heating system

The heating system is another excellent area for upgrading. Inefficient old boilers waste a large proportion of the energy fed into them, whereas new condensing boilers are around 90 per cent efficient. Replacing a boiler needn't be a disruptive task and can be done cheaply and speedily. Investigate options for upgrading the rest of the heating system at the same time such as installing high-efficiency radiators, thermostatic radiator valves and modern heating controls.

Aim to make your system as simple as possible with easy-to-operate controls and clear instructions for users. When selecting a heating system, keep the following questions in mind:

- how are the occupants supposed to use the controls?
- how would my staff and I use the equipment?

Optimum start/stop and weather compensation controls are now mandatory in new buildings, so it's useful for you and your staff to learn how to use them. Installing them in existing buildings will also provide benefits. Optimum start controls 'learn' the heating performance of your building, switching on heating at the last moment and off as early as possible to maintain comfortable temperatures during periods when the building is occupied.

Weather compensators are energy-saving tools that improve the efficiency of your system. These measure external temperatures and adjust the temperature of the water in your heating system accordingly. So, on cold days, radiators will be hotter than on milder days. Other controls can detect longer-term changes in daily temperatures and switch the system off for the summer.

Where electricity is used as the main form of heating, you may want to investigate the use of renewable energy or changing to a cleaner fuel type.

Green roofs and walls

An idea which has been around since the Hanging Gardens of Babylon but has made a rapid comeback in the last few years is the green roof. A green roof has some sort of vegetation growing on it. There are two kinds: intensive and extensive. Intensive green roofs are more substantial and are usually found on large commercial buildings. They also have a more significant impact on the structure of the building than extensive green roofs. Extensive green roofs use thinner growing media and require a lot less maintenance.

Green roofs offer many benefits. As an extra layer of roofing, they provide insulation and waterproofing. You'll find your building temperature is more evenly regulated and you are less likely to experience leaks. On top of this, they provide some health benefits through cleaner air, as well as sound insulation, more biodiversity in the area and aesthetic benefits.

Green walls have a planted outside façade and a cavity between the inner and outer walls. They provide similar benefits and help to reduce the need for heating and cooling costs, particularly in industrial buildings.

Green roofs and walls require some care during their installation, so we recommend that you contact an expert to help you plan, install and maintain them.

Help

■ Livingroofs is an independent resource on green roofs in the UK. Visit the website (www.livingroofs.org) to get advice and help in locating your nearest green roof expert.

Renewable and low carbon technologies

We discussed renewable tariffs for energy in Chapter 2, but have you considered producing your own energy on-site? This requires some investment, but many new-build developments around the country are required to have some form of on-site energy production from renewable technologies, so we are beginning to see more of these. While these technologies can be expensive, they do offer financial paybacks in the form of reduced energy bills and payments from an energy supplier if you sell electricity back to the National Grid. As fuel bills increase, these technologies will become increasingly affordable.

Renewable technologies can produce both heat and electricity, so think about which of these you need and in what quantity. The heat producers include:

■ **solar water heating** – this transfers the sun's heat to your water heating system;

- **biomass boilers** – an updated form of the caveman's campfire, these burn wood or other organic materials to produce heat, and require a nearby source of biomass to keep transport emissions to a minimum;
- **heat pumps** – these use either the warmth in the ground or air for your heating system and work even in cold temperatures; they rely on electricity to run the pump.

For renewable electricity, the main technologies available are:

- **photovoltaics** – again, these use the sun, but this time the light creates an electric field across a layer of molecules (typically silicon) which causes electricity to flow;
- **wind turbines** – these are high-tech windmills in which the rotating shaft generates electricity;
- **hydro** – these are mini-versions of big dams; an environmental assessment is required to ensure you don't affect the course and wildlife of the river.

There are a couple technologies that produce both heat and electricity:

- **combined heat and power** – this is a mini-power station which can run on fossil fuels like natural gas, or biomass. When producing electricity, huge amounts of heat are taken away through cooling towers. By capturing and using this heat, it becomes a much more efficient way of producing electricity, particularly for manufacturers which have high heat and electricity demands.
- **anaerobic digestion** – bacteria breaks down organic material in the absence of oxygen, producing methane biogas, which can be burnt to produce electricity, heat or both. The technology is particularly applicable to businesses that produce large amounts of organic waste in the form of food or garden waste, manure or industrial waste water.

Not only do you have to consider what type of energy you need, you have to know what 'renewable resources' are available to you. Technologies that rely on the sun work best when oriented towards the south and on a particular tilt, so some roofs are more suitable than others. Wind turbines obviously need wind, but they work best in a strong, steady wind and aren't so good in big cities where the wind gets chopped up by other buildings. All these technologies have some limitation or requirements to make them work better, so take these into account. By using the right renewable technology, you can maximise the amount of energy it provides, which will give you a better return, both financially and environmentally.

Think about the times of the day or night when you want to use your energy. You'll want to use the energy as it's produced, particularly with electricity-generating technologies. For instance, if you run a bakery and many of your working hours are during the dark, a solar technology probably wouldn't make sense. By using the electricity at the same time you generate it, you will take a larger chunk out of your fuel bill by not using your energy supplier's electricity. You can get a tariff from most electricity suppliers that will allow them to buy back any electricity you produce, but the rates they offer are lower than what they charge you, so it makes sense to use as much of your renewable electricity as possible.

The savings for carbon emissions run in parallel with this. Most of the electricity we get from the National Grid comes from fossil fuels and the process is pretty inefficient. However, some of the inefficiencies arise because the electricity has to be transported from the power station to your business. Therefore, using electricity you've produced on-site leads to a greater reduction in carbon emissions.

This doesn't mean that you can only use electricity produced while you are working. Obviously some of it will be sold back to the grid and you can opt for a system that stores electricity in batteries. However, this will cost you more and make the system less efficient.

For all the above technologies, find out whether planning permission is required from your council. In most cases, it will be.

As you can see, there are many elements to consider when installing this type of technology, so if you're serious about this purchase, we recommend you get an expert to assist you. In some cases, it's advisable to ask a consultant to produce a feasibility study on which technologies would be best for your business. In other cases, you may know which technology you need, but an expert can help you to decide where it should be located. If the latter applies, a reputable installer can help with this. You can find an installer through the various trade associations.

- British Wind Energy Association: www.bwea.com
- Combined Heat and Power Association: www.chpa.co.uk
- Solar Trade Association: www.solar-trade.org.uk
- Heat Pump Association: www.feta.co.uk/hpa/index.htm
- Renewable Energy Association: www.r-p-a.org.uk

Case study

Miller Research (UK) Ltd is a small economic research and sustainable regeneration consultancy based in North Monmouthshire in Wales. The business has a strong commitment to sustainability and ethical trading. But, as much of its work involves travel to relatively remote communities across the UK, the company was concerned about its carbon footprint. Partly to redress this, it has installed a wind turbine. Not only will the turbine reduce the company's carbon footprint, but it will also bring added benefits in terms of cost saving and offer a radical statement to clients about the business's commitment to sustainability.

Getting the turbine

Miller Research opted for a 'Proven 6' from Proven Energy because it offered a mixture of track record, UK engineering and a size which roughly met the business's needs. The Proven 6 is rated at 6kW which means it produces between 6,000 and 12,000 kWh a year. It took almost two years from inception to project completion and initially the company struggled to obtain a quote for installation. Eventually it settled on Green Earth Energy, a local company based in Pontrilas, Herefordshire.

The planning department in Monmouthshire proved helpful and gave the company tips on completing the application forms. Planning was granted within two months and there were no objections from any of the neighbours. In fact, most were very supportive and some even asked to buy into the project.

Paying for it

Miller Research was unable to obtain a grant from the government's Low Carbon Buildings Programme, as it was oversubscribed at the time, or an interest-free loan from the Carbon Trust. However, it was in a position to finance the project, which cost £25,000 in total, out of its own funds.

Miller Research has estimated that it will save about £800 per year on its electricity bill if it uses about 60 per cent of the 11,000 kilowatt hours that the turbine should generate. On top of these savings, the company will receive a payment from its energy supplier, Ecotricity, for every kilowatt hour it generates, regardless of whether Miller Research uses it or if it is exported back to the National Grid. The reason for this is that the government requires that energy suppliers generate a certain amount of renewable energy through the 'Renewables Obligation', so suppliers are willing to pay a premium for renewable electricity.

Miller Research chose to stay with Ecotricity as this supplier had just doubled the amount it pays to small generators of renewable energy. In total, Miller Research expects to receive almost £1000 per year from Ecotricity. Adding all this up, the company has estimated it will save £1800 a year and that the turbine will pay for itself in 13.8 years.

The turbine went up in the second week of June 2008 with a launch party attended by the Welsh Assembly Government's Sustainability Minister. Since the turbine has been running, it has acted as a demonstration project for the local community and the company has had a lot of interest from farmers in particular, who are especially concerned about rising energy costs.

Help

■ For basic information on renewable technologies and how they work, check out the Carbon Trust's publication 'Renewable energy sources technology overview', which you can find by searching the website: www.carbontrust.co.uk.

SPECIFYING A NEW BUILDING

As a result of government initiatives and improved standards in the building industry, progress is being made towards more sustainable buildings. The government has made a strong commitment to improving the Building Regulations so that we will have zero carbon new homes by 2016. It has also committed to making all other new buildings, including commercial and industrial ones, zero carbon by 2019. In the meantime, local councils have stepped in to try to bridge some of the gaps. Many areas now require a certain percentage of energy for new developments to come from renewable sources built into the development. In these 'Merton Rule' policies, named after the London Borough of Merton which started the trend, the amount of energy from renewable sources usually begins at 10 per cent, but some councils will be seeking as high as 40 per cent in the future.

So, while our commercial buildings are improving as a result of planning and building requirements, there is still much that can be done to make them better. So far, this chapter will have given you a good idea of the types of improvements that can be made to existing buildings and measures to bear in mind for new ones. However, to make a big impact, you need to work closely with an architect or building designer, so choose one with the right level of sustainability experience and know-how.

The Association of Environment Conscious Building (www.aecb.net) can put you in touch with architects in your area who have an interest and experience in sustainable building. From the start, you should make it clear that you are interested in sustainable criteria for your building, particularly if there are certain aspects that you value over others. We also recommend that you look at the client guides available on the Commission for Architecture and the Built Environment (CABE) website (www.cabe.org.uk), which you'll find under its 'services' section. In particular, the main guide, 'creating excellent buildings', will help you to understand the role that you need to play as the client. The CABE website also has a number of useful case studies to give you ideas of the type of building you might want to build.

Specifying sustainable business premises

If you are in the privileged and currently rare position of being able to buy or rent a new building and also to determine its specification prior to being built, it is important to be clear on your expectations and take care to select the right designer or architect. That person should not only be clued up about sustainability issues but be willing to work closely with you in trying to identify your needs in order to reach a clear specification. Only then will it be possible to create a truly green building which meets your needs in the short-term and is future-proofed against changing economies and climate.

Approach

It is usually best to work from a design approach first before establishing the details in the design, so start with zero carbon, zero waste, zero water, etc. Taking a tough approach like this can result in different and superior design solutions than starting with the Building Regulations and making incremental increases from there. When designing in this way, it is useful to review the key aspects of sustainable features which will ultimately represent a good overall building design.

Sustainability principles

The following 8 'L's represent important sustainability features which are neither exclusive nor prescriptive, but should provide a good platform on which to determine and refine your specification. The first five are drawn from research carried out by the University of Kingston and the latter have been added by the authors of this book.

- **Low consumption** – minimal consumption of resources (energy and water) when the building is in use. A zero emissions approach would embrace this concept and also work to generate its own energy and collect water from the building or site as well.
- **Low impact of consumption** – having embraced the first feature (e.g. energy and water efficiency), this takes account of the environmental impact of residual resource requirements, e.g. any energy that staff need to use should come from a renewable source.
- **Low impact building** – this principle recognises the environmental impact of the materials used within the building, in particular the energy embodied within its production, whether this relates to raw materials extraction, transport, processing or packaging. It should take into account the effects of disposal, as well as the toxins released

through its lifetime. Also, the social impact of the building should be considered. This principle should also be extended to all aspects of the specification, including interior fittings and maintenance regimes for instance.

- **Longevity** – this principle recognises that the building is fit for the purpose (or a range of purposes) for which it was designed. Or at the very least, it should require minimal effort to change its use for a particular tenant or purpose. And it should be designed to serve that purpose for a significant period of time. Therefore the specification must recognise changing climates, e.g. stronger winds, higher flood levels or higher (or lower) temperatures. This feature is not just about a long lifespan. Short-life buildings should be designed for easy disassembly and reuse of major components.
- **Location** – the estate agent's mantra is here further reinforced by sustainability. Ideally, your workplace will be close to where staff live and accessible to public transport and community facilities.
- **Low health impact** – this principle is designed as an antidote to the widely recognised and commonly experienced sick building syndrome. This addresses comfortable temperatures, adequate humidity and air quality, access to natural daylight, and user-controlled ventilation and lighting. Often missing from specifications is the issue of low-toxin materials and limited use or absence of materials which will absorb and retain toxins. Attractive views and use of indoor plants are important factors, too.
- **Loosefit** – while it is difficult to predict future usages for a specific building, the specification should build in flexibility and recognise that the building's use will change over time. For instance, having a building with fewer internal structural walls will enable interior spaces to be more readily changed. Also by building in cabling or plumbing for future installations, the building will become more future-proof and less prone to redundancy.
- **Loveability** – usually missing from specifications is the concept of beauty. Though residing within the eye of the beholder, there is every reason to create enjoyable space and buildings through good design. This will help to maximise the usefulness and usability of the building over a long period of time. It could be argued that an ugly building, an inappropriate setting or poor internal layout can not be truly sustainable.

Passive design

Passive design principles are an essential part of good ecological design. This means making the most of the shape, layout and construction of the building to minimise energy consumption. Passive design will reduce the energy needs of the building and the size and cost of *active* systems for heating, lighting and other energy services.

Passive approaches can be employed for the following features.

- **Heating** – passive heating relies on windows to provide an effect for buildings just like in a greenhouse, whereby the sun is used for warming the interior. Generally the larger the south–facing windows, the greater the warmth you will get from the sun. Also, using building materials with a high thermal mass will help to absorb this heat and limit internal temperature fluctuations.
- **Cooling** – passive cooling can work in two ways: firstly by limiting how warm the building gets and therefore the need for cooling and, secondly, by using the shape and layout of the building to create more airflow as internal temperatures rise. Reducing demand for cooling can be done in many different ways, such as by utilising energy-efficient appliances whose main source of waste energy is heat and by shading against excessive heat from the sun, e.g. by using light shelves or louvres on windows.
- **Ventilation** – the passive stack effect is the main means of natural ventilation, but this could be assisted by solar or wind energy. The stack effect works when air rises through the building as it is heated by its occupants and any equipment or machinery. As the hot air escapes through the vents or windows at the top of the building, this draws fresh air in from the bottom.
- **Lighting** – optimum use of natural daylight is essential in reducing demand for electrical lighting. Not only does this lead to lower running costs, but it often provides a much better quality of light. Windows are the main means of achieving this, but these could be supplemented by daylight tubes and roof lights. Light coloured and reflective surfaces will also help.

Cooling and ventilation are clearly linked and, together with lighting, often represent the biggest energy users for many businesses. A passive approach to these areas can make the biggest savings to your future energy bills.

In all cases, it is important to recognise that just because the energy is 'free', it is not necessarily obtained easily. So, passive considerations need to be carefully integrated within the design at an early stage and not added as an afterthought. Incorporating passive features in the design will make the building's shape, orientation and internal layout work to best effect.

The easy way?

The Building Research Establishment has developed an Environmental Assessment Method, known as BREEAM, that takes a holistic approach to building design. BREEAM looks at the following categories and assigns credits for more sustainable approaches to:

- management
- health and wellbeing
- energy
- water
- transport
- materials and waste
- land use and ecology
- pollution

These credits are added together and given weighting to produce one of four ratings, from 'pass' to 'excellent'. It is recommended that you aim for 'excellent' as this will add the most value to the building. If necessary, though, you should accept a lower level if certain aspects prove not to be feasible or outside your budget. If used early enough in the process, this approach can be used as a design tool when it will be easier to meet a certain standard. Using the assessment in later stages will usually result in adding on features to gain higher scores.

BREEAM assessment can be used for a range of different building types, including:

- offices
- retail
- industrial

More information can be found on the Building Research Establishment website: www.breeam.org.

Determining a specification

Whether you choose to aim for a zero carbon, zero waste building or look to the Building Research Establishment for guidance on sustainability, you will need to work with a designer or architect to develop a specification for your building. Keeping in mind the principles described above, follow these three steps to develop that specification.

1 First, articulate your needs for the building as best you can to provide an outline specification of what you want from the building. This need not be in technical language, but it should express the intended purpose of the building and contain all attributes that you consider either essential or desirable.
2 Next, speak to two or three designers face to face, ideally ones who have already designed the type of building you are proposing. Recommendations or references are a good way of finding the right person. This conversation is an opportunity to explain your intentions and outline specification and establish how you might work with them to agree a more detailed specification and, later, an acceptable design.
3 Finally, select a preferred designer and develop a specification for agreement with them. In this specification, you should agree milestones and fees as well as examine possible hurdles and issues that might come up and how they might affect the design and timetable.

RECOMMENDED LINKS

For more information on what you need to do to be awarded an Energy Performance Certificate for your building, go to the government's Department of Communities and Local Government website: www.communities.gov.uk/epbd.

Sustrans provides a wealth of information on cycling, including maps and routes, which can help you find the ideal location for your business: www.sustrans.org.uk.

The Carbon Trust has a wide range of information on how to reduce your energy needs, including specific help for lighting and renewable technologies: www.carbontrust.co.uk. For more information on specific renewable technologies, speak to the relevant trade association:

■ British Wind Energy Association: www.bwea.com
■ Combined Heat and Power Association: www.chpa.co.uk
■ Solar Trade Association: www.solar-trade.org.uk
■ Heat Pump Association: www.feta.co.uk/hpa/index.htm
■ Renewable Energy Association: www.r-p-a.org.uk

The British Fenestration Rating Council (BFRC) has an excellent searchable database of windows on its website: www.bfrc.org.

The Livingroofs website is an independent resource on green roofs in the UK: www.livingroofs.org.

When looking to design a sustainable building, visit the Association of Environment Conscious Building website (www.aecb.net) and the Commission for Architecture and the Built Environment website (www.cabe.org.uk). You can find out more about the readymade Building Research Establishment Environmental Assessment Method at its website: www.breeam.org.

Index